GROWING UP
THE HARD WAY

GROWING UP THE HARD WAY

Grace W. Thomson

Order this book online at www.trafford.com
or email orders@trafford.com

Most Trafford titles are also available at major online book retailers.

Printed in the United States of America.

ISBN: 978-1-4669-0293-0 (sc)
ISBN: 978-1-4669-0294-7 (e)

Trafford rev. 11/02/2011

 www.trafford.com

North America & International
toll-free: 1 888 232 4444 (USA & Canada)
phone: 250 383 6864 ♦ fax: 812 355 4082

TO MY HUSBAND MATT, ENCOURAGER, CRITIC
AND FRIEND, MY SON, MY DAUGHTER AND
THREE GRANDCHILDREN AND, LAST BUT NOT
LEAST, MY BROTHER JOHN FOR HIS MEMORIES
AND HIS HELP IN WRITING THIS BOOK.

INTRODUCTION

I'm leaving bonnie Scotland today with my future mother-in-law and flying to Canada. With profound sadness I'm leaving this land of my birth but I hope I never have to return. This rugged country with its purple heather covered mountains and deep bluebell glens is beautiful beyond belief; however, I knew if I was ever to have any kind of life I had to get far away.

Let me tell you the story of my family and perhaps you'll understand.

CHAPTER ONE

My Dad was the son of an Irish bigamist drunk. His father, David Gibson Thomson, deserted his first wife, changed his name and fled to Glasgow, Scotland. Grandfather was a laborer and worked at the brush factory owned by my grandmother's family. He was a man of spit and polish and was able to impress the owner's only daughter Elizabeth, who was the company's secretary; with his smooth Irish blarney brogue.

I'd like to marry Elizabeth," said the slick Irishman.

"You must be joking! I'd never allow my daughter to marry the likes of you," replied her father aghast at this man's blatant arrogance.

"Well," replied the conceited bigamist. "You'll have to let me marry her because she's pregnant."

"Get to Hell out of my house and take the stupid bitch with you!" gasped the ruddy faced father.

"Tis a hard man you are brother. Haven't we walked together on the 12th of July with the Orangemen?" David continued his proposal thinking he had an ace by playing up the Orange Lodge a group of Protestants who celebrated together. This organization had been in existence for centuries since William of Orange won the Battle of Boyne in 1690 against the English King James 2nd, a Catholic. The group, when they marched, could cause riots in the streets. Bigots would be one way to describe them but they were convinced that they were within their rights and retained their long held belief that the Catholics were inferior.

"Orangeman indeed, I'll be resigning from the lodge as soon as possible; so I'll never have to look at your ugly mug again. Now take her and go!" With a determined stride the father walked from the room.

Holding the weeping Elizabeth by the hand David said, "Don't cry my love your Dad will change his mind once he sees the bairn."

A quick trip to the Registrar Office and the false David Gibson Thomson and the lovely luckless Elizabeth Johnston were married. They continued to hope her father would relent and make his new son-in-law a partner in the thriving business. The reconciliation never happened and Elizabeth was condemned with my father and his younger siblings, yet to be born, to a life of abject poverty.

The family moved to Greenock, Scotland, a town supported mainly by shipbuilding, a sugar refinery and a distillery. James Watt, the inventor of the separate condenser for the steam engine, was born in Greenock and this discovery was so significant that it is credited with bringing forth the industrial revolution. Massive tonnage of vessels were built and launched from Greenock. Submarines, ocean liners, naval ships and cruise ships were built by

Scott's Shipbuilding and Engineering and the Greenock Dockyard. The Queen Mary and the Queen Elizabeth were built at John Brown's Shipyard and proudly launched into the River Clyde by royalty.

The family rented a room and kitchen in an attic of an old tenement of flats. Throughout their marriage my grandmother was pregnant yearly and gave birth to thirteen children with only nine surviving to adulthood.

"That's my space and my blanket," argued young David as he pushed his sister away from the fire. Grabbing the threadbare blanket he curled up in a fetal position and held his hungry stomach.

"Why do you get the only blanket and sleep close to the fire?" cried his sister Peggy.

"Because I'm the oldest, the biggest and I stoke the fire!" David replied emphatically.

The kids flopped where they could find a space mainly on the floor with old coats for blankets. The parents slept in a large closet called a set-in bed. During the early 1900's indoor plumbing was a luxury, known only to a few, and a chamber pot was used and carefully carried down several flights of stairs by young David to the outdoor toilet every morning.

"This piss smells of beer!"

Last night his father had been heard vomiting yesterday's booze. The boy carefully carried the stinking pot down the chipped and worn-out stairway to the toilet, slopping the contents on his clothes meant he had to wear the stained garments to school until they were washed in the communal washhouse once a week. The entire tenement of over thirty used the outside toilet which had a door of wooden fence slats that allowed the cold and rain inside in winter and stunk in summer because nobody would accept the job of cleaning it.

"Hold onto my shirt tail Jean," instructed David.

Jean was his youngest sister and his job was to take her in the morning to the toilet when the chamber pot was full. The cistern had a chain hanging down and small children had to jump and swing on it to flush and it was perpetually broken. Toilet tissue was too expensive; so, David carried an old newspaper ripped into squares. A black backside from the newsprint was the norm.

Back in the room a fire was burning to dry their laundry and cook their food. Coal was something they could ill afford and anything that would burn was stuffed into the grate under the blackened soup pot or the kettle constantly boiling for stewed tea. Soup was a staple food and usually contained a large bone devoid of meat added to any vegetables that could be scrounged from the greengrocer.

"Is there anything to eat?" David asked hopefully. "I have to walk to school and I'm hungry."

"There might be some crusts of bread, that's all," replied his mother. "Maybe today I can get something from the grocer on credit".

David attended the Ardrossan Primary School for six years, during that time half his day was spent sewing sandbags for the troops fighting World War I and the remainder of the day he was given a rudimentary education. Because he was the oldest child it fell to him to leave school and find a job, at twelve years of age David would become the sole bread winner of his family. His father was seldom sober and unable to find or keep a job.

"I've got a job at Mr. MacLean's greengrocer shop," said David jumping with joy. "Now I'll be able to help feed us."

The neighborhood grocery store was the ideal place to work where he would deliver groceries and be paid with food. Every day, except Sunday, David walked barefoot over wet and slippery cobblestones pushing a heavy two-handed flat cart delivering groceries to the richest families of Greenock. The cart was designed for two boys to push but because David was tall for his age the stingy grocer decided one was enough.

"Take that load to the west end," instructed Mr. MacLean. "Make sure you don't crack any eggs."

David hated delivering to the rich who lived in spacious mansions guarded by large dogs that were trained to bite all trespassers. He grew to despise all dogs and suffered many bites from their slobbering fangs.

The maid answered his timid knock.

"What are you doing at this door you dirty little beggar. Can't you read? It says NO SOLICTING," David, who badly needed glasses, squinted at the notice.

"I'm not soliciting miss, I'm delivering." David wasn't sure what soliciting meant but he knew it did not apply to him.

"Didn't anybody ever tell you to go to the servant's entrance?"

"No Miss, I wasn't told by Mr. MacLean," David whispered.

"Well you know now. You're type can't be seen at the front door of this posh house." The maid said proudly as though she owned the house.

David dragged the cart to the back door and was promptly dismissed. Tips were never given and his wages were stale bread, bruised fruit, cracked eggs, or anything the stingy greengrocer could not sell. Meanwhile, his father having decided his eldest son was caring for the family was gambling the dole money on the dog racing, drinking alcohol and; occasionally, working as a horse racing bookie, a job he felt suited his status as a man-about-town. Any money he earned was quickly spent treating his alcoholic friends to a round of whiskey. Every night David's task was to find him when he was flush with cash and to convince him to keep some of the money for his large hungry family. The boy got to know every smoke filled pub in the neighborhood where his father hung out with his Irish Paddy pals. Alcohol came to signify for him poverty and he vowed to be a teetotaler for life.

One night, as he helped his intoxicated father stumble home, his alcoholic parent decided magnanimously to treat his son.

"Can you tell the time?" asked his father, as he swallowed, belched, and spat out every word.

"Yes," replied David skeptically and wondered why his father cared.

They stopped at H. Samuel's the jewelers and his father pointed to an 18 carat gold watch in the window.

"I'm going to buy you that watch," said the boozer to his amazed son.

This was a valuable gift and it became a God's send to the family. The watch was pawned often and redeemed whenever possible and the shillings were spent on necessities to help his brothers and sisters.

David was fortunate and had a dark blue suit which was kept for church and every Sunday morning it was ironed, before attending services, to crack and kill the fleas hiding in the pants cuffs. His mother played the church organ, when she wasn't obviously pregnant, and this enabled her son to join the Boys Brigade where he advanced through the ranks and became an officer. Poor people could not afford a seat in church and the only way they could possibly attend was to join a church group that usually met in an adjoining building. Children were taught to fear the wrath of God. Hell, fire and brimstone were preached to the young attendees. John Knox's Scottish Presbyterians were a dour and strict group of worshippers and pragmatic to the point of miserable stinginess. David discovered another group of worshipers called the Plymouth Brethren that served tea and scones after services and decided to join. This did not last long he found that the dry scones were as hard to swallow along with their brand of religion.

"You're Mum is dead," said Mrs. O'Malley, the midwife, in a monotone voice. "She died in her sleep."

David stood by his mother's bedside and was totally mystified. "I don't understand. What happened, what did you do?"

"I didn't do nothing. I didn't even notice she was dead, I was reading the newspaper," said the dirty faced slatternly woman who was calmly picking at a scab on her chin.

David looked down at the blood soaked bed and sobbed even in death his dear mother was beautiful. She lay there white faced, her long black eye lashes resting on her cheeks, her pale lips that he had kissed so many times were drawn tightly shut as though grimacing in pain. David bent over and gently kissed her cheek and brushed her hair with his fingers back from her forehead it was disheveled and soaked with sweat, obviously from a long labor. He wanted to slap the slovenly, slack faced midwife, he could feel the rage burning inside but he knew it was useless. Mrs. O'Malley was a neighbor who sat in as a midwife when there was no money for a doctor.

His beloved mother having known only a life of privilege before her marriage could not survive this poverty stricken life. She was age forty when she died giving birth to her thirteenth baby she had slowly bled to death. They named the baby Johnny and he quickly became the favorite brother.

Money for the funeral was unavailable; so, David decided to walk twenty miles to Glasgow to his grandparent's house to ask them for money to bury their daughter. He found their opulent home and bravely rang the bell. An angry maid answered the door.

"We don't give to tinkers;" she said sharply.

"I'm not a tinker. I've come to see my grandfather," David replied confidently.

"Rubbish, Mr. Johnson doesn't have grandkids," she said.

"You're wrong, I'm his grandson."

"Wait there," she ordered.

He could hear the maid telling someone about the stranger at the door. Footsteps, and there stood his maternal grandfather. He was an old man with white greasy hair, yellow skin that hung in folds on his flaccid face, and tight thin colorless lips. His mother, when alive, bore no resemblance to this creature. He stared at David blinking repeatedly as he examined the young man.

"So, you're the son of the bitch!" His bitter words were fired at David like bullets.

David was dumbstruck, how should he answer this verbal assault on his beloved mother?

"Yes, I am sir," said David in a clear voice.

David knew he had to be careful not to offend this obviously bitter old man, but to hear his dead mother called a bitch cut him to his core.

"What do you want?" The old man leaned closer to David and he could smell his putrid breath.

"My mother is dead grandfather and I need money for a coffin and a plot." David explained.

The outburst from this miserable creature exploded so swiftly that David was forced to step back out of the old man's reach as he attempted to strike him with his clenched fist.

"I'll not give you a penny to bury that worthless woman. I don't care if you dump her body in the garbage," and, with this outburst, the door was slammed in his face.

Nothing made sense to David as he wearily walked the twenty miles home. The one thing he felt certain of was that his alcoholic father had basically kicked his mother to death without raising his foot. This time his watch was pawned to pay for his mother's funeral.

Standing alone he watched as workmen prepared a paupers grave for her.

"Stop blubbering and hold an end of the rope," said the dirty faced workman as he thrust the rope into David's hand.

Gripping his end of the rope he could feel it cut into his palm but he was determined not to drop his mother, David stooped to allow the cheap plywood coffin to be lowered into the hole.

"Okay let your end go," ordered the workman and, with that done, he pulled the muddy rope up from the grave.

He stood there alone as the workmen threw lumps of wet mud on the box, this sound hurt him more than all the cruel words he had ever suffered. In order to find her grave from the rows of unfortunate souls resting in peace he placed a pile of large rocks at the site and, starting at the cemetery's long driveway, he paced toe to heel counting until he reached her graveside. He visited her grave for many years although; unfortunately, other paupers were probably placed on top of her, burial spaces were costly and the corporation didn't waste any space on the poor.

Nevertheless, in spite of the poverty, David survived and served four years in an apprenticeship with an engineering firm and was taught to be a turner. A turner works a lathe and constructs small parts for ships engines or, in David's case he later made the gyroscope for torpedoes at the Royal Naval Torpedo Factory for World War II.

CHAPTER TWO

David, when his mother died, was twenty-one and had the burden of supporting his eight siblings but he was soon to meet the woman who would pull him up by his bootstraps from his life of poverty.

My Mum, Grace Florence Blythe Williams, met David Thomson, my Dad at a house party which he was coaxed to attend by his sister Isabel. Mum was named after two English heroines, Grace Darling, a lighthouse keepers daughter, who rowed out to save shipwrecked sailors from drowning and Florence Nightingale, the famous nurse of the Crimea war who was instrumental in starting the career of nursing. Mum spent most of her childhood in West Sussex, England in the picturesque village of Upper Beeding. Her father was born in Cardiff, Wales and named Charles Arthur Thomas Blythe Williams, he was the only son of a Welsh professor of languages. After the death of his mother he ran away from home and joined the navy. During his time in the navy his ship docked at Greenock, Scotland and he met and married a Scottish girl named Margaret McQue. After World War I the couple settled in Sussex, England and had eight children. He was a bargeman on the River Adur working for the Beeding Cement Works and when he was laid-off they decided to move back to Greenock, Scotland where he might find work in the shipyards. Just three of the children moved with them the remainder of the family stayed in England, except the two eldest sisters who were sold as indentured servants and were shipped off, one to Canada and the other to the USA. Nina, the sister who went to Canada was never seen nor heard from again. Maggie, named after her mother, went to the USA and; eventually, ran away from the farm, where they treated her like a slave, and joined the circus. The only job available to her was riding a motorbike on the Wall of Death, this contraption was a gigantic cylinder and it involved her travelling at a breakneck speed thus enabling her to stay on the wall. She did this for many years but decided that it was too dangerous and bought a hoopla stand, this venture made so much money for Maggie that she was able to buy a farm. Her first husband a World War I vet infected Maggie with syphilis she quickly divorced him and later married a Quaker. They settled down and lived peacefully in Sioux Center, Iowa.

Poverty was also an unwelcome bedfellow in Mum's home. Her father worked cleaning the filthy bilges of the ships and, after a gash on his elbow became infected, he slowly died of blood poisoning. Mum left school at fifteen years and worked at three jobs to support her mother and two siblings. Her morning job was at Dr. Osborn's office, a dentist, whose main practice was with the seamen from the many ships docked at Greenock. She was paid to hold down the drunken sailors while the dentist extracted teeth sans anesthetic. In the afternoon she washed the eggs at the local egg market and became quite adept at gently cracking several eggs to give to the poor. Her evening job was at the bakers where she became the supervisor in charge of loading a fleet of vans for the early morning deliveries. Here too the local poor came to know the English girl who could always find "stale" bread to give away free. Within a short time she was able to resign from her first two jobs when she became the manageress in charge of a large chain of bakeshops. Her sister Ruby refused to work and spent Mum's hard earned cash which was generously doled out to her by her mother. Mum resented the way she was treated at home and retained this anger throughout her life she did not suffer laziness or stupidity in any form and blamed her mother for Ruby's behavior.

When David met Grace he fell in love and would have no other girl, she attempted to discourage him many times and would leave him heartbroken at the bus stop while she travelled home; nevertheless, he courted her in his plodding way and they were married at the Registrar Office. Their first child, a daughter, was stillborn because my drunken paternal grandfather scalded my Mum with boiling water while he was attempting to make her tea when he stumbled causing the entire contents of a boiling kettle to scald her very pregnant belly. The baby was born prematurely and stillborn and that was the last time grandfather was ever allowed into our home. My twin brothers Duncan and Angus were born in a tenement attic. The joy of my Mum's life! My maternal Granny was the midwife and when Angus, the second twin, was born he was quite blue and showed no signs of life; meanwhile, my Mum exhausted after a long difficult delivery lay quietly stroking her feeble baby lying beside her. Granny was certain he was stillborn until quite suddenly she saw him move; so, they started rubbing him more firmly until he let out a weak cry. The twins were the favored children and were greatly admired; therefore, Mum tried several birth control methods. Two children would have been the ideal family because they could barely make ends meet and work was almost impossible to find during the 1930's. Dad was laboring as an assistant to a bricklayer because he could not find work at his trade.

The tenement attic proved to be a dreadful home, freezing cold in winters and unbearable hot in summer, added to this was the fact that my mother had to drag a twin pram down and up the stairs to the attic every time she went shopping, going shopping with this monstrosity required the strength of Goliath. They moved from the attic and rented a row house in Orr Avenue where John was born and labeled mistake number one. John began his adventurous and mischievous life early and before the age of four he was found one day with his head stuck between the rod iron railings that surrounded the row houses. It was a mystery how he had managed to fit his head between the bars and no amount of pulling or twisting and great gobs of Vaseline could set him free; eventually, welders had to be called and the iron bars removed. Shortly before I was born, and labeled mistake number two, they rented a bigger house in a working class neighborhood. The exact date of my birth is unknown because April 18th was my drunken grandfather's birth date and April 20th Hitler's birth date and, since I was born at home, they decided to register me with another date. Renting this house was a stroke of good fortune because the first house offered to them was obliterated when the Greenock blitz began. The house was semi-detached and we lived in the bottom half, our neighbors the Blair's lived upstairs. The house had a living room, an eat-in kitchen, a master bedroom for my parents, a bedroom for the boys but no bedroom for me I slept on a pull-out couch in the living room and in the cold winter months it was the warmest room in the house. Before going to bed Mum banked the fire up with coal dross and it glowed all night, coal was already rationed because of the threat of war and my brothers walked the railroad tracks looking for it; occasionally, a kind hearted stoker would throw out several shovels of coal to the waiting boys as the train rumbled past. The main bonus for us in our new house was we had a front lawn and a drying green for the washing, which was reduced in size to accommodate an air raid shelter, and a good sized vegetable garden. We grew potatoes, beans, turnips, carrots, cabbages, peas, turnips, spring onions, radishes and ruby red rhubarb and the harvesting of our vegetable garden helped save us from starvation when the threatened war began. When World War II broke out we were the only family in our street to have our front lawn dug up, the other wives were aghast at this destruction of the landscape and could not tolerate having their lovely green lawns and rose gardens destroyed. Mum and Dad realized we would need every scrap of food to survive and our Victory Garden was a testament to the honest Scots who never stole from us.

CHAPTER THREE

In 1939 World War II began and Britain was thrust into a hellish war. Scotland too was about to share in the misery and my brothers and I were to know hardships for which we were ill prepared.

The Greenock Blitz began in May 1941 when the Luftwaffe attacked. Two successive nights of intensive bombing practically destroyed the small town. The raids targeted the ships and shipyards, but like the Clydebank Blitz, another town on the River Clyde bombed the previous March, the brunt of the bombing was taken by the citizens. The shipyards were valuable the workers were expendable. Air raid sirens at 12:15 am started the bombing, incendiary bombs were dropped around the perimeter of the town. The distillery was set on fire, providing a huge beacon for the rest of the bomber force. The second wave dropped parachute land mines which caused widespread destruction.

I was in my bed, awake and petrified by the sound of the bombers that swoop and dived like gigantic black bats over our house. I could not move I was petrified.

"Get up Grace!" yelled my Mum. She yanked the rough army surplus khaki blanket from my shaking body.

"I need to pee," I cried.

"No time, the bombs will soon be falling!" Mum dragged me from my warm bed and bundled me into my siren suit. The suit was like an overall and covered me from head to ankles.

I grabbed my Mickey Mouse gasmask and pulled it over my face. Wearing my boots on the wrong feet I wobbled out of the door and down the steep steps and stumbling in the dark I ran behind my Granny. I staggered and groped my way through the Victory Garden. My three brothers pushed me over mounds of wet muck towards our shelter. It was impossible to see until suddenly a bomb hit a nearby building and flames leapt into the air like gigantic orange and red tongues licking skyward.

My Dad and the neighbors constructed our Anderson shelter, it was a crude structure and definitely unable to withstand a direct hit from any bomb. The shelter was dug deep into the ground and as we slithered down the wet muddy steps, I jumped over puddles and squeezed into the dark, dank room. The stink of candle wax and cats pee assaulted our nostrils. We huddled together like frightened mice in this dark dank tomb and waited for the air-raid to begin. It was no mystery to us why the German's were bombing our town because we had numerous industries that were assisting in the war effort, the Clydeside area workers made ammunition, submarines, torpedoes, ships and, on the east side of the Clyde, hidden under huge mounds of grass were oil tank storages.

Granny lit our stumped candle. We sat on wooden benches and adjusted our ill fitting gas masks we looked like aliens gasping inside the masks and peered out of the eye piece. Granny and Mum did not wear their masks and refused to listen to our complaints about the contraption. When we whimpered our dislike of the mask they reminded us of our neighbor who had been gassed in World War I and went around gasping for air the remainder of his miserable life.

"Ouch!" My backside was once again pierced with slivers from the rough bench.

The noise of the bombs exploding and the drone of the planes made it impossible to sleep so we stared wearily in the dim light and shivered in the icy cold. Mum had dumped old khaki blankets that scratched our skin and itched. The pillows were damp and were covered with black and grey institutional ticking. We couldn't lean back on the shelter walls because they dribbled with dampness. John secretly removed his mask and was gathering hot tallow candle wax and popping it into his mouth. My brothers teased John and said he had a stomach like a goat and would eat anything. Poor John, a growing boy, was perpetually hungry. Granny had her eyes tightly shut and her hands clasped in prayer.

"Hail Mary Mother of God Pray for us Sinners," Granny had started her click, clicking on her rosary beads. When Granny married Grandpa she stopped going to Catholic mass but after his death she reverted to her old ways. This was the only time I ever saw Granny praying and she certainly was a first class Catholic. The entire process was a mystery to me but she seemed to have a direct connection to God. Mum called her the crisis Christian. I didn't care what she was doing I knew her chanting soothed me and I sidled closer up to her.

Granny was generously endowed with soft comfortable curves and appeared to me to be a series of rounds. Round head, round glasses that slipped down her round little nose and fell when she snoozed onto her decidedly round tummy. I enjoyed snuggling up to her warm body. She was an affectionate woman and gave us the love that my Mum seemed unable to give. Granny seldom removed her apron and it always had an aroma of food from her cooking. Her little hands were pudgy and when she sat by the fire she placed them on her tummy and twirled her thumbs back and forth, I noticed that she did this a great deal when trouble was brewing in the Thomson household, the act seemed to soothe her.

Throughout the bombing this gentle woman called out her entreaties to God only stopping to catch her breath and to call out of the dark shelter to her daughter.

"Good God Gracie, come inside!"

"Damn the fear of it. I want to watch the bloody bombers," shrieked Mum.

"You'll get hit. Shrapnel is falling all over the place," pleaded Granny.

Mum was a slim woman with coal black hair and brilliant blue eyes that flashed with anger, she always seemed ready to strike. I rarely saw her fists unclenched a habit that probably began when she arrived as a teenager in Scotland. Scottish children were brutal to the English kids; unfortunately, they were taught how the cold hearted English defeated them at Culloden and massacred hundreds of the brave highlanders. The highland clearance was a favorite subject of the teachers and they taught us how the bloody English herded the unfortunate Scots into coffin ships and sent them to the colonies. They dreamed of another William Wallace who would chase the English back across the border. Mum fought with almost every neighbor and was called a Sassenach bitch. The name was hissed at her like a spitting angry cat. This is a derogatory name given to the English by the Gaelic inhabitants. She was reticent to be friends with our neighbors because of her experiences in school and, as she saw it, through no fault of hers she was born in England and reluctantly brought to Scotland. Because of her early treatment by bigots she always yearned to return to sunny Sussex.

"Damn you Hitler! "Why are you so determined to kill us?" she shouted with her fist clenched tightly and raised skyward.

The bombs were so near they were causing our ears to pop and, as we waited for this torture to stop, we silently prayed that there would not be a direct hit on our "shelter" because this place would definitely become our tomb.

Finally, the All-Clear sounded at 3:30 a.m. and we crawled out of the shelter to see the destruction. The town was ablaze as the whiskey from the distillery was a river of fire. Little did we know that 200 innocent civilians were dead and 1,200 badly injured. Countless homes were destroyed and some of the shops had suffered a similar fate.

Next morning we were anxious to explore, John especially wanted to see if the school had been bombed.

"Look at this chunk of shrapnel it must be twelve inches long," John was proudly holding up a piece of metal with a string attached. We had no toys and searching for pieces of shrapnel was to become a new pastime for my brothers.

"Dad said the incendiary bombs had parachutes," he was bounding like a deer over the destruction hoping to find the perfect piece.

John hoped to find an unexploded incendiary bomb and, should he find one, he believed he'd become a hero when he reported it to the Home Guard. Dad, when he was not working the nightshift, took his turn defending our shores as a member of the guard. Mum was thankful he was too old to be conscripted.

"Let's go to the dam, I heard they are fishing for bombs there," John encouraged us.

To reach the dam we climbed over broken glass, wood and slates. My brother's gave me a piggy-back ride because I had trouble climbing over the rubble, they are responsible for my welfare Angus and Duncan were eight years older than me. As we clambered along we could see our world had been considerably changed. After the bombings and the destruction of the roads I seldom had skin on my knees or elbows. My knees were perpetually scabbed with cuts and bruises caused by falling over rocks and tripping into holes, bandages or sticky plasters were unavailable; so, most cuts healed and left small scars. One cut on my elbow became so infected that it required a boiling hot poultice to draw out the puss. I always felt that Mum enjoyed her role as a nurse and bragged that she could endure most blood and guts. To make matters worse if we played outside at night we had no street lights and we fell often; throughout the war our town was in black-out and we were hoping to God the bombers did not return. Every window had dark blinds and they had to be drawn and not a chink of light could be seen on the outside and a fine was imposed on anyone breaking the total black-out.

When we reached the dam the Home Guard and firemen were fishing for bombs. The men were dropping grappling hooks into the water and hoped to pull out any unexploded bombs.

"Let's watch them," said John. "They might catch one and it'll explode and blow them to bits."

"You kids there," yelled one of the firemen. "Bugger off!"

We stood back and watched from a distance hoping to see and hear a gigantic explosion. The firemen stuck a pole into the ground with a notice reading "Danger" and left. The dam where we once fished for tadpoles was now unsafe.

The only place left untouched was the cemetery and we're not allowed to play hide and seek between the tombstones. This never bothered us because there's a deep lily pond at the bottom of the cemetery and a gigantic green monster lives there. If we ever paddled in that water the monster, probably as big as the one in Loch Ness, would grab us with his fangs and drag us into his underwater cave. My brother's were strong swimmers but I was afraid of the water.

"Let's climb to the top of the hill, we can probably see the whole town from up there. We'll be able to see where the whiskey poured through the town and burned everything in its path," called John as he galloped ahead of us like a pony.

We climbed to the top and far off in the distance flames were still leaping from some buildings and others were blackened shells but, much to our dismay, the school was still intact. Better luck next time Adolf!

After our adventures we ran home to wait for Mum she had gone off to see if any of the shops were open and selling food to feed her hungry kids. Long queues usually formed at the dairy and the butcher's shop. It was slim pickings for the waiting mothers but they were grateful for whatever was available.

"Bread and a little milk was all I could buy, it'll have to be bread pudding to fill your bellies," Mum said sadly.

"Yuk!" we chorused.

"Go to bed!" she demanded. "That'll teach you all a lesson for complaining."

That night, as we tried to sleep, nothing made any sense to us as we listened to our empty stomachs growling. Hunger sucks!

CHAPTER FOUR

School remained open throughout the war and it was a cheerless place. We were taught by spinster ladies who wore their long black college graduation gowns and looked like gigantic ravens as they floated through the hallways. They appeared to really despise kids and punishment was generously applied by means of a broad belt with a slit up the center providing them with two snake-like tongues to torture us. We were required to bring our gas mask and if we forgot it we were belted. Because of the war we had no writing paper or pencils, every child must bring a slate, chalk and a rag to clean it. Spitting on the slate was forbidden; also, a broken slate was forbidden and again punishment was meted out. Children should be seen and not heard. No laughing, running, hopping, jumping or skipping. The students must always walk close to the wall the teachers must be allowed to pass unimpeded; so we called ourselves the wall-walkers. We must not touch the teachers and were made to feel dirty. Dirty kids were the norm because soap was rationed and we tried to use it as little as possible—not a problem for most kids. Caustic carbolic soap was used to wash our clothes on the scrubbing board, scrubbed the outside steps, inside floors, bathed us and shampooed our hair. A special bar of black Zulu soap was kept to kill lice or fleas should we ever be unfortunate enough to pick up the cooties.

Miss Charmers was the primary grade teacher, she was an extremely nervous skinny wee woman, her eye had a tic and she perpetually rubbed her red nose. Her mouth was pursed up like a prune and her forehead was permanently crisscrossed like a road map. A pair of wire rimmed spectacles perched precariously on her thin nose but they do not appear to really help her see the lessons printed on our slates. Grey hair came early to this sad woman and it was screwed into a tight bun. School for the teachers was a drudge with little or no supplies their tempers were quick to flare at the least little infraction. The only book available was the teacher's copy which was tattered through years of use. The Bible was on the teacher's desk and every morning religion was generously doled out. We sat in Miss Charmer's class afraid to move. Bathroom breaks were forbidden we must attend to the call of nature before coming to school or at recess. The toilets were broken, dirty and disgusting; however, when we had to go the boys would piss-up the back wall, the girls would rush into the toilet, pinch their nose, relieve themselves, scoot outside and gasp the fresh air.

John disobeyed every demand from his parents or teachers no matter how often he was strapped and slapped or punched he refused to cry. His school days were torturous! In class it was demanded that we sit still and when John found it impossible she promptly produced a hammer and nails, kept especially for fidgets and nailed the sides of his pants to the chair.

"John, tell me how did you rip your pants?" Mum demanded.

"I caught them on a nail," John lied.

"There must have been at least four nails to cause all this damage," said Mum.

John stood quietly waiting for a slap and looked at his torn pants. In order to prolong the wear of his pants the rear had a large patch the size of his backside. The sides now had four thumbnail sized ragged holes. He knew he was in trouble.

Again he lied to avoid punishment, "I caught them on a fence."

"I don't know how I'll mend these holes. I've a good mind to let you go out with a bare backside. Get out of my sight!"

John ran for his life and would gladly have gone naked than submit to more punishment.

Clothes were rationed and every garment was made from old coats, sweaters or dresses. When John arrived home with tattered pants it meant she had to go to the Salvation Army store and look for any old garment she could rip out and make him new ones.

June arrived and school was over for the summer. We were ready for fun on the hills and burns surrounding our home, but instead we were told we were to be evacuated to the country and would not be spending any of the summer holidays at home because the Luftwaffe may decide to bomb Greenock again.

"I don't want to go," protested John. "Bobby Faulconer's uncle has a farm and I'm going there to work."

"You're not going with Bobby and that's all there is to it," said Mum.

"The Luftwaffe aren't coming back here there's nothing left to bomb."

"How the hell do you know," said Angus. He was always the brother in charge and bossed us around like a regimental sergeant major. He had a violent temper and several times it was beyond his control, he was known to bite ears in a fight. One day an unfortunate boy fought him and lost the tip of his ear. It was never wise to argue with Angus, he was volatile.

"You mind your language you're going. You have no choice," demanded Mum.

After the first bombing the Luftwaffe returned the following night and evacuation of children became a necessity. Like ugly black birds they swooped and dove down to make certain they killed the workers who lived close to the banks of the River Clyde. The houses lost almost every pane of glass from their windows. Dad was working in an underground bunker close to the Battery Park making torpedoes and as we huddled in our shelter listening to the bombs we wondered if he would be safe.

Next day John and I sat on our doorstep waiting. Angus and Duncan had once again gone off looking for shrapnel.

"Is he late?" I asked.

"Yes, but that's okay he probably worked overtime," John replied.

Our eyes were trained to the corner of the street as we waited patiently for the sight of a lone cyclist, our Dad, coming home. Suddenly, we saw him guiding his bike carefully over a sea of glass to avoid a puncture to his tires.

He was alive! He was home! An explosion of happiness burst out of us bigger than any bomb! Suddenly, the window in the kitchen was thrown open and the white lace curtains flew out like a flag. Mum was watching and waiting.

That afternoon my brothers went swimming in Caldwell Bay when, once more, the sirens started to wail. The only shelter available was in the ritzy part of town, they made a beeline for one but when the three shivering boys tried to enter they were barred at the door. Peering inside they could see it was partially empty and several dogs were being kept safe.

"Go away, you can't shelter here wearing your wet swim suits," declared the toffee nosed swank.

Shivering and shaking the frightened boys ran to the sea wall and crouch behind it for protection. When my father heard of this he was furious, once again he was reminded of how he was treated as a boy by the so-called upper class. Some things never change.

It was decided that the Thomson children were to be evacuated to the country. An identification tag was pinned to us and we each carried a small bag with our clothes and gas masks.

"We're going to a farm," said John happily.

"How do you know," snarled Angus.

"Well, if it's in the country that's where they have farms."

We were sent to a village called Laurencekirk. Mum gave us no kisses goodbye, no hugs and not a single word of love, she did not believe in any public display of affection nor did she exhibit any private display. We were growing up the hard way. Her main goal in life was to keep an immaculately clean house and she was a tyrant to cleanliness. The hall in our house was polished to a mirror like shine so much so that when walking up the hallway you had to be especially careful you didn't slip and break bones, touching the wall was forbidden. The kitchen, she bragged, was clean enough to eat our meals off. The front steps were scrubbed weekly and a stone cleaner was smeared on each step to give them a white appearance. We climbed up the banister rather than step on them, a mark on a step led to a cuffed ear and the chore of reapplying the stone whitener. With her four messy kids gone her house could be pristine.

"Now you behave yourselves, work hard and don't cause any trouble. I'll come back for you at the end of the summer or when they feel sure there'll be no more bombs," said Mum and left us.

It was a small village and we were placed in the butcher's house. He was a plump jolly fellow and smelled of lamb chops; obviously, he was not suffering the deprivation of rationing. He had a round tummy and a couple of chins and nodded in agreement at everything his wife said. His wife made it very clear that she did not enjoy the chore of caring for four hungry children and clicked her tongue at us every time we entered her kitchen which was her domain. The Thomson kids were trouble with a capital "T".

We were expected to be quiet at all times except when we had chores. Duncan and Angus were to work at the nearby farm, news that caused John to sulk and he was immediately tagged as a trouble maker and given extra chores. He was to weed the flower and vegetable garden; also, he was to turn the mangle handle on wash day, this antiquated contraption required a great deal of brute strength which was no problem for John because he was a sturdy boy. After the clothes were boiled in a boiler they were fed between two rollers and the handle was slowly turned to squeeze out the water. Many small fingers were caught in the rollers and no safety panic bar could be pushed to release the grip, squeals of pain from the child and the rollers were quickly reversed and the fingers were once again crushed on the return roll.

When this task was done he was to fill the bucket with the coal from the bunker. When he finished all chores he had to scrub the kitchen floor because, according to the butcher's wife, he was responsible for all the dirt trekked into the house.

I was expected to set the table for all meals and to help wash and dry the dishes. Being the youngest and only girl I was thankfully excused from all hard work.

Luckily, we were allowed to go to church on Sundays and to have time off for good behavior. We were sent to the kids classes and if we could memorize and recite passages from the Bible we were given highly prized mottos these were little stickers of angels and saints with religious quotes for Christians to live by. I desperately wanted a collection of the stickers. We were not greeted warmly by the other kids because it quickly became obvious that our knowledge of religion was poor, attending church in the Thomson household was not encouraged since my Dad had decided to divorce himself from all things religious. Dad chose agnosticism as his creed and hard work as his calling. It began when a minister of the Church of Scotland asked him to pay for John's christening; unfortunately, the minister was intoxicated and allowed John to slip from his arms into the font. My parents were not regular attendees of the church they needed every penny they earned to feed their family and the church was thriving without their help; hence, when the collection plate was passed they had nothing to contribute and this was frowned upon when they offered coppers; consequently, they quit going.

John and I escaped the village church out the side door. Duncan stayed because whatever Angus did he followed him like a sheep. Duncan was considered the sweet unassuming child and was a favorite of the adults. I thought he was a sneak.

John and I headed for the farm where we discovered cages of ferrets and; assuming, they were pets John opened the wire door and set them free. Out they jumped and made a mad dash heading straight for the ducks and hens.

"Grab their tails," shouted John.

"I can't they're too quick," I yelled.

We had a great time chasing the agile little creatures across the farmyard.

Charging out of the barn and brandishing a sharp pitchfork the red faced farmer tried to catch us.

"I'll kick your backside for letting those pests out," yelled the farmer. "Don't you know that ferrets are pests not pets? You're not kids from the village, where do you live?"

We reluctantly told him that we were evacuees and the look on his face told us that we were to him displaced persons.

As a punishment we got no food from the butcher's wife and were sent to bed with a growling empty stomach. Our fondest wish was to go home but it wasn't hard to figure out Mum was glad to be rid of us. Granny had gone to England to be with her other daughters and Mum had the summer off without the burden of four kids.

John had made friends with a local boy and spent a great deal of his time playing Cowboys and Indians. Angus and Duncan worked at the farm and, as I had no playmates, I lounged on the couch reading a book. We had almost no books at home we had an old bible, a dictionary and one book "How Green Was My Valley". My Dad encouraged us to read this book because he considered it an excellent example of the working man's struggle against their bosses.

Dad had been approached by the socialists to join their party but because he had no money for dues he declined. He was a strong believer in unions and insisted that his children join one whenever they had a job.

We spent our days in Laurencekirk trying to amuse ourselves and to stay out of trouble. The butcher had a shed at the bottom of the garden for his tools we explored it looking for anything to amuse us. Toys were nonexistent but we were hoping for an old ball.

"Look at this," said John to a village boy.

He held up a box of Swan matches.

"Let's go to the woods and we'll have a campfire," said John.

I was having an afternoon nap when the sound of the fire engine came clanking throughout the town.

"My God, the German's are invading! They've bombed the woods and set them on fire, soon the whole town will be ablaze. Where's my gas mask?" The butcher's wife was running like a frightened rabbit, lifting cushions and pushing me aside in an attempt to find her mask.

Eventually, John and his new friend were found trying to stamp out the blaze and were dragged by the scruff of their necks by the police back to the house.

A letter was promptly sent to our parents demanding that they come quickly to collect their unruly children.

CHAPTER FIVE

Since returning home we seldom see Dad, he works the night shift and has become a quiet intense man. Lately, a perpetual scowl has caused deep lines between his eyes and his cheek bones stick out prominently from his face. His red hair is falling out and a bald spot has appeared on the top of his head; probably, caused by poor nutrition. He now has thicker glasses because his eyesight is failing as he engineers the very detailed parts of the gyro; also, his skin is sallow from long nights working underground and seeing sunlight only when he cycles home. He bought an old bicycle and he rides home instead of wearing out his only pair of shoes walking. The war has worried and aged him. We missed Dad in the evenings playing his harmonic, he was self taught and could play any tune we hummed to him, he especially loved the old Scottish verses written by our bard Robert Burns. We used to sit by the fire, before the war, and he would play and we would sing all the old songs.

My brothers were all accomplished harmonica players but I could never master the blow and suck technique, I always had too much saliva and slobbered into the instrument.

Rationing was taking a toll on all of us and we were skin and bones we were living on vegetables from our Victory Garden with very little protein; occasionally, Mum bought liver and it was probably the least favorite of the food she was able to buy at the butchers. I chewed on so many stalks of rhubarb that my bowels were causing me to scurry to the toilet. Bread was rationed and my brother John was perpetually hungry because he ate his share and looked for more, he was scolded for scrounging food. Mum dare not send John to the bakers because he was known to eat the soft inside of the loaf as he walked home and punishing him was a waste of time. I found a source of food it was a little tree that grew at the bottom of our garden, I called it "My Little Bit of Bread and No Cheese" tree. Every day I chewed the leaves and they filled a hungry hole in my gut. I would not dare eat the vegetables from the garden this would be considered greedy. I tried chewing on the soft tar bubbles that popped up on the road on hot days but my teeth and tongue became black and I was punished for my stupidity. A pal told us that the roots of thistles were quite tasty but in order to reach them we had to pull up the jaggy weed and this was definitely not worth the pain. The thistle is the emblem of Scotland and it is supposed to protect us from all enemies. The superstition dates back centuries, no one knows how it began but our teachers told us that when Scotland was attacked by the Vikings the invaders came barefoot and stepped on the thistles, let out their cries of pain and awoke the sleeping populace. Scotland won the battle and adopted the thistle as its lucky emblem. The Irish have the shamrock for luck and the Scottish have their thistle; unfortunately, for the two countries the English did not believe in lucky weeds and felt entitled over the years to invade both countries.

Superstition is common among the Scottish and Irish and my Mum has adopted my Granny's superstitious ways and was convinced that she had special powers, she told us that being the seventh daughter of the seventh daughter she could bless or curse people. Mum believed that if someone did her or her family wrong she could put a curse on their head. I came to believe she could when I saw the evidence. A workmate was causing problems; so, she put a curse on him that he would break both his legs and, very soon after her curse he broke his leg in two places. I suppose the curse had a minor flaw because she was greatly disappointed and had hoped he would break both legs and be bedridden. My mother had the power to frighten the daylights out of me. She also liked to read teacups and told endless stories to hapless women at parties and was credited with matchmaking some of the oddest couples. In one case she told one silly female that her true love would be a man with one leg. One legged men were common after the war; so, it wasn't difficult for the gullible woman to find a mate.

Summer ended and we have been spared from more bombings. This was hardly surprising because the bombers had almost destroyed the small town and most of the workers. The west end of the town was spared, the east suffered. The factories were still operational and Hitler probably had decided when he won the war they would be an asset.

School began in September and we have no new clothes. I have a pair of hand-me-down shoes from my brother John they're scuffed and worn out because he kicked at anything that wasn't nailed down. Daily, I stuffed cardboard inside the shoes to keep my socks from wearing out but when it rained my feet were always wet and cold. I had a pair of Wellington boots for wet weather but they too had a hole I tried; unsuccessfully, to seal the boots with the wax that Dad used when he sealed envelopes. Eventually, Dad bought a cobbler's last and repaired our shoes. I had two pairs of navy blue knickers, one woolen jumper knitted from an old sweater, one skirt and some cotton dresses made from washed out threadbare sheets. My Mum had managed to buy an old army coat from the Salvation Army store, ripped it out and made me a coat. We are lucky because Mum bought a Singer sewing machine and paid it off at sixpence a month, now she sews all our clothes from any material she can scrounge. A sewing machine was definitely a necessity for a growing family. I was allowed to help her when she ripped apart the seams of old clothes. Woolen sweaters were picked apart and I rolled the wool into tight little balls. By the age of ten Mum had taught me how to sew and knit my own clothes. Our neighbor Mrs. White worked at a factory canteen and when Mum sewed or repaired her clothes they bartered. She gave us sugar, flour or dried eggs for Mum's work and she was given some of our clothing coupons. Mrs. White considered herself a snappy dresser and rationing clothes for her was worse than food rationing. Dried eggs were a God's send because a family was allowed one egg per person per week but usually only one per fortnight. I was given the top of a boiled egg with no yolk I definitely did not have to worry about clogging my arteries.

A group of new kids were enrolled in our school they were the children that survived the bombing but their homes did not, they now live in the old army huts deemed too dilapidated for the military but useful for the homeless.

The families were destitute and had nothing except the clothes they were wearing the night they lost their homes.

One day a thin dirty little girl arrived in our class.

"Who will share their slate with the new girl?" asked the teacher.

My hand shot up.

"Please Miss, I will."

She sat beside me and I could smell pee from her ragged clothes, her hair was matted and her dirty face was scratched and bleeding, her red nose had green snot plugging her nostrils, cold sore scabs surround her lips and they had obviously been picked and were bleeding. I placed the slate between us and as we leaned over our heads were touching.

"What's your name?" I whispered.

"Jenny."

That night I paid dearly for my generosity. Mum was a stickler for cleanliness in all things and at bath time, when she was washing my hair, she let out a screech.

"Good God lice! Get me the small toothed comb."

This comb, with teeth so fine that nothing could escape it was raked across my scalp, my head was scratched until it bled and then it was lowered into the sink and unbearably hot water was poured over it until I cried out in pain. Mum clutched the Zulu soap and started rubbing the ghastly black bar until it foamed into a grey paste as it penetrated the shafts of my hair to kill the beasts. I squeezed my eyes tightly shut because the caustic bubbles stung like battery acid.

"Lean your head over the newspaper and I'll comb it some more," she demanded.

I watched and saw the lice fall.

"Quick, catch it! Those things can jump higher than a double decker bus," yelled Mum.

Fingers were grabbing for the elusive lice as they cavorted over the paper almost joyous to be free. One after another they fell on the paper my hair had obviously become a hatchery for the bugs. Mum grabbed and cracked them all between her two thumbnails the adult lice could be easily removed but the nit eggs still clung to my hair.

"We'll have to shave her head, it's the only solution," said Mum to Granny.

My Dad had a straight back razor the blade was sharpened on a strap and he; occasionally, sliced his face and walked around with little pieces of paper soaking up the blood. I had vision of my head covered in tiny bits of paper.

I watched my wet hair, combined with my tears, fall onto the bathroom floor. I was bald! She left me with a tuft at the top and a place for my pink elephant clip Aunt Susie gave me for my birthday, at least with the clip I wouldn't be mistaken for a boy.

Next morning I refused to go to school.

"You're going and I'm taking a matchbox of dead lice to show that teacher," said Mum grabbing a wee box.

John held my hand and whispered, "I'll punch anyone in the mouth if they make fun of you."

The teacher was shocked when my mother arrived with her package.

"I know Mrs. Thomson it's a problem I am constantly cleaning my scalp to keep the pests away. What would you suggest I do to keep Grace free of lice?"

"Sit her alone," suggested Mum.

So began my year of isolation, I sat in class an outcast; meanwhile, Jenny blithely played with everyone and unconsciously spread her bugs throughout the school.

At lunchtime I was joined by John and his friend Bobby who clearly felt sorry for me. We ate our sandwiches and drank the free milk supplied by the government we were; also, served a daily dollop of ghastly cod liver oil and concentrated orange juice to prevent rickets and scurvy. All meat and fish were rationed; so, lunchtime was bread and jam or beetroot sandwiches. The jam was made from the brambles we picked in the autumn the beetroot from our Victory Garden.

Food was becoming scarcer because the German U Boats were sinking any food we might receive from the USA or Canada.

One day a truck loaded with ripe red apples arrived at our school marked Apples from Canada. We all know that Canada is part of the British Empire and we were over the moon with joy at being so lucky; however, before we were given an apple by Mr. Davis, the headmaster told us we had to sign a thank you note he had written to the kind Canadians. I had never tasted a juicy apple, we do have rock hard green apples growing in a nearby garden but if we are ever caught stealing them we are severely punished; truthfully, we don't care they have been the cause of a severe belly ache or the runs.

The Canadian apples were handed out one by one to the kids, and we could eat them immediately or take them home. I chose to take mine home to show my Mum. Big mistake! Every school has at least one bully and we were no exception.

"Give me that apple!" demanded Morag.

Now Morag was a huge girl and three years older than me; also, she had the reputation of winning every fight she started.

"No!" I yelled emphatically.

I started to run but it was useless she soon grabbed me and threw me to the ground and I was trapped between her fat legs. Morag, an only child, was obviously eating more than her share at home; nevertheless, I held onto my apple and managed to squirm free. I ran into a nearby garden and dived between the rounded rows of potatoes. She found me. Desperately, I managed to wiggle from under her, twisted around and with one hand grabbed her long pig-tailed hair and pulled, she was howling like a banshee as she tried to twist free. I had never needed to fight because, having three brothers they did the fighting for me; however, a free apple was worth fighting for and I was determined to keep mine. Mrs. Grierson, the owner of the house, saw us in her Victory Garden and came out to see what the ruckus was all about.

"She's trying to steal my apple," I gasped.

"You pair get out of my garden and go on home," admonished Mrs. Grierson.

That day, I had victory in the garden and fighting for what was rightfully mine was exhilarating. If the allies fight like I did they will win the war. I sat on my doorstep and with a pair of dirty hands and muddy face I devoured my apple to the core. Mum, looking out of the kitchen window just smiled.

Oh! Canada I thank you.

CHAPTER SIX

"He should be buried like a pauper just like my mother. That drunken swine didn't even have the decency to turn up to see where they buried her," said my furious Dad.

My grandfather died of cirrhosis of the liver. Dad did not attend his funeral his sister Peggy, who was married to a baker named Noel, was quite rich and had a crystal chandelier in her dining room. Very posh! They owned a string of bakeries throughout Glasgow; so, she took care of all the funeral arrangements. Peggy, who had fewer bitter memories of her father than Dad, buried him with wreaths of flowers and an expensive coffin. Dad never spoke to Peggy again.

Throughout his life Dad never touched alcohol he was a 100% teetotaler he despised liquor and even on Hogmanay, a celebration in Scotland at New Year, he drank only non-alcoholic bramble wine made by mother. Drunks were common in Scotland and every Friday night after pay day they would fall onto the buses spewing their booze all over the floor. They staggered and fell into passengers and guiltily thrust coins at the kids, I was never allowed to accept their pennies because Dad would shove them away and with rage tell them to take their money home to their own kids. He hated pubs and their owners and blamed them for most of the poverty in Scotland. When I was a teenager this hatred would directly cause me problems when I dated young men.

Shortly after grandfather died Uncle Johnny came to live with us, we adored him he worked at the Central picture house and allowed us into the pictures free of charge on Saturdays to join the ABC Minors. The kids would burst their lungs singing the song:

> We are the boys and girls well known as Minors of the
>   ABC/
> And every Saturday all line-up to see the films we love
>   and shout allowed with glee/
> We love to laugh and have a sing song what a happy
>   crowd are we we're Minors of the ABC/.

We sat in the Gods (the balcony) where the stink of tobacco smoke, left over from the previous evening, stung our eyes where we watched Roy Rogers and his wonderful horse Trigger, The Dead End Kids and the Three Stooges. Dad bought a second-hand cine projector and he was able to show us Mickey Mouse and Donald Duck cartoons and sometimes Charlie Chaplin, he projected the films on a canvas screen. Dad would roar with laughter when he showed Chaplin, especially when poor starving Charlie cooked and tried to eat his boot. He especially enjoyed

Charlie when he worked like a maniac trying to keep up with his job in a factory.

"Sometimes I feel like poor Charlie he's definitely the little man against the world," sighed Dad.

Once a month we had films at our house and we invited the neighborhood kids. Mum put a collection box at the door and the contributions went to the Lifeboat Society, this charity helped seamen. We played reels of old movies Johnny had borrowed from the Central picture house. The only drawback on picture night was the lack of something to munch because sweeties were rationed and we were allowed two ounces a week and this did not last long. Angus managed to keep his the longest by always buying humbugs, a rock hard boiling, he would stash his away and if he needed us to do a chore for him he would bribe us with a humbug. Those humbugs and toffees were the cause of many a toothache.

Uncle Johnny stayed with us until he was eighteen and was called up to serve in the British Navy, Dad advised him to join the Navy because he figured he might be safer there than in the trenches. Johnny chose to sail on a wooden minesweeper to make extra money because by then he had a girlfriend he hoped to marry.

We saw him only once after he sailed away he brought us gifts, toy soldiers for my brothers and a china doll for me dressed in satin. I was delighted and cherished the doll but; unfortunately, the doll was very fragile and the first day I owned it I tripped on our high stairway and smashed her head. My brothers glued its head together and stuck curly wood shavings on its skull to look like hair. It was truly ugly! Johnny promised he would bring me another the next time he was on leave. He never came home again.

We were playing outside and saw the telegram boy cycle past us and, when he stopped at our house, we knew it was serious because telegrams were seldom sent and any time one arrived it was bad news.

We heard Dad's whistle calling us home. We have a special whistle and we always responded to it.

The four of us sat on the couch looking up at Dad as he stood by the fireplace, the unwelcome telegram was in his hands.

"I have bad news," said Dad. "Johnny is missing and presumed dead."

Mum was bawling and mopping her face with a handkerchief. Dad's face was ashen and twisted in pain.

I cried out, "Does that mean he isn't coming home and I'm not getting a new doll?"

I felt a sharp dig to my ribs and I was told to shut up.

We were sent outside so that my parents could be alone to console one another. As we sat on the steps we could hear them both sobbing.

"What does it mean presumed dead?" I asked.

"Stupid, it means they can't find any bit of him he was blown to pieces," said Duncan. He always considered himself the brainy one of the family and listened only to classical music on the BBC radio.

"A wooden minesweeper clears the sea of mines and sometimes when it is loaded with mines it can hit one and boom!" John explained.

Our house was a tomb after Johnny died, I sat on the cold stone stairs and waited for him to bring my doll, I refused to believe he was dead I figured if he was just missing they'd find him. For weeks I waited for Johnny to come home, my Mum saw me there and did nothing to relieve my misery.

"Maybe he'll be found swimming in the Mediterranean Sea he's a really strong swimmer," I rationalized.

John found me waiting endlessly for my uncle and the promised doll, hugged me and whispered.

"Forget it Grace he's not coming home."

Soon after the news of Johnny's death I came home and found the house empty this was strange because Mum was always there for us. I went upstairs to ask our neighbor Mrs. Blair if she knew where my Mum had gone.

"No Grace I don't."

I sat outside by the vegetable patch and absent mindedly picked at weeds and waited; eventually, I saw her in the distance walking very slowly home.

"Where were you?" I asked.

"I went to see my sister," she said quietly.

This was unusual because ever since my Mum was a teenager she had never gotten along with her sister she considered her lazy. She must have been desperate for a place to go to have visited Aunt Ruby.

That night I heard her explain to Dad why she ran from the house and left her laundry scattered all over the kitchen floor.

"I was standing by the kitchen sink and I felt someone tap me on the shoulder. I turned around and there stood a vision of Johnny. He was smiling and dressed in his white naval clothes," explained Mum.

"I'm all right Gracie," said Johnny's ghost.

"I almost collapsed. I pulled off my apron and ran for my life."

Now Mum might believe that she was the seventh daughter of the seventh daughter and could cast spells but she definitely did not believe in ghosts.

Months later a little box with medals for Johnny arrived with a short note of condolence. The note thanked my father for Johnny's service to his King and country. Dad tossed them in the drawer and spat out his rage.

"Damn them! What part of this country did they give Johnny? He's not even buried in Scotland!"

Life in our house was quiet for sometime after Uncle Johnny went missing and Dad continued to worry about his other brothers and sisters. Uncle Sam was a member of a Scottish regiment and wore a kilt he was fighting in North Africa. A German named Rommel, the Desert Fox, was there and considered one of the smartest generals in their army. The English Field Marshal Montgomery was having a wicked time trying to defeat him. Uncle Robert was in a better place he was in the British Army stationed in England and was a cook. Aunt Susie and Aunt Liz were working in a factory making bullets and Dad worried there might be an explosion.

Mum's only brother Jock was in the Merchant Navy and she was extremely proud of him. During Dunkirk when the British were badly defeated he, and other men, had been responsible for saving the lives of many soldiers when they waded out into the channel to be picked up by the waiting boats. Many of the young soldiers were loaded down with guns and backpacks and could not swim. Jock was a strong swimmer and jumped into the water repeatedly pulling the exhausted boys out of the water. He was now in the Atlantic Ocean attempting to bring supplies to Britain and was in great danger from the waiting U Boats.

CHAPTER SEVEN

Greenock was now the major port for sailors and they came by the thousands. Sailors disembarked from the USA and the main thing on their minds was women of any shape or size. We also had French sailors they were distinguished by a little red pom-pom on their beret. The French sailors had nothing for the kids but the Yanks were sure generous.

"What's wrong with that man's face?" I whispered to my Mum.

I was staring wide-mouthed at a tall black sailor smiling down at me. We did not have black men in Scotland and this was quite a surprise to me that they also had American black men who were as tall as trees. We were taught that the black men lived in Africa not the USA.

"Sorry, she's never seen a black man before," apologized Mum.

They were everywhere when we walked to school they stopped and asked us if we had an older sister.

"No I don't, but can you give me some gum chum?"

We thought we were talking Yank talk asking for gum chum and every time we met a sailor we would ask for chocolate or gum, the sailors had a ready supply for the kids, but the main attraction for the older girls was stockings. Stockings were rationed and the young women used to draw a dark pencil mark up the back of their legs to look like the seam of stockings. The older women wore thick bullet proof stockings—beyond ugly.

When the American sailors docked the women from Glasgow and surrounding towns came in droves.

"Whores, that's all they are," said Mum.

"What's a whore?" I asked.

"I'll explain it to you one day."

Life was changing all about me and I'm sitting and watching without a clue and nobody would explain, nothing made any sense to me anymore. You're too young to understand, don't ask so many questions, children should be seen and not heard. This was my mother's mantra all designed to keep me ignorant.

To me the whores looked pretty all dressed in party clothes with long dangling earrings and bright red lipstick as they clip clopped through the town wearing their high heeled shoes and giggling as they held onto the arm of a sailor. The local women in their threadbare mended drab dresses and pale faces were worn out and tired. War had been unkind to the local girls as they worked in menial factory jobs.

At tea time I announced that when I grew up I'd have pink cheeks, red lips, high heeled shoes and colorful clothes just like the whores, I wanted to be happy and go dancing nightly.

Mum jumped from her seat and hit me a hard slap to my head I landed on the floor with my meal spread all over me.

"Don't you ever say such a disgusting thing again!" she yelled. Unfortunately, my Mum failed to understand that a child only saw beauty in the pretty young women and I was unaware of the sad side of their lives.

The town did not have much to offer the sailors, the shops that still existed were bare and the only other amusement available was dancing or liquor. Scotland always had an overabundance of pubs.

When the kids walked to school every morning the road beside the cemetery wall was littered with white balloons, I thought I had discovered a new source for toys that the sailors had thrown away.

"Don't touch that!" yelled Angus

"Why not, it's just a balloon?"

"No it's not!" he screamed in panic as I picked one up. "I'm warning you, if you don't drop that thing I'll slap you. They're dirty the sailors wear them on their pee-pee they call them condoms, we call them French Letters."

Angus and Duncan were fourteen years now and understood grown up things.

"I don't believe you. They don't look like a letter they're made of rubber I'm going to ask Mum. Why would the French sailors leave weird letters all over the road?" I protested.

That night I asked if I could have some of the white balloons I had seen by the wall.

"No you can't and when you're older I'll explain the reason. Right now you're to consider them poison."

Once again no explanation was given.

The word poison was enough to convince me to leave them alone, it was hard to believe that these clean-cut young men could bring poison to Scotland. They also drew the eyes and nose of a funny little man on every wall that read "Kilroy was here" This man Kilroy was peeking at us all over town on the railway station wall, the church wall and the cemetery wall. He sure got around!

Eventually, we could not play beside the cemetery wall because the sailors there were making love to the local girls, my brother Angus called them the wobbly kneed bunch. Again I did not understand.

The young woman went wild for the young handsome American men but; unfortunately, for many it did not turn out well. The local men and the workers from Eire who came to Scotland for work, had problems accepting the sailors and fights broke out at the pubs and dancehalls. The MP's and the local police had a steady of job of arresting drunks.

Our neighbor had a teenage daughter, a very pretty girl, she was engaged to marry a British officer, but the temptation was too much and she started to go dancing with the American sailors. Nightly, we saw Isa skip down the stairs on her way to a dance.

One day John and I returned home from school and were confronted with what looked like a massacre.

Blood! Blood! Blood everywhere! Great gobs of the stuff it was all down our outside stairs. At first, we thought Mum had attempted suicide she had been threatening to off herself for months. Was this the blood that had poured from Mum's slit wrists? We stood at the base of the stairs stunned and uncertain.

"What do you suppose happened?" I asked.

We stepped gingerly up the stairs trying to avoid the blobs, went inside and couldn't find her. Panic stations!

"Let's go ask Mrs. MacKenzie she might know."

"You're mother is at the hospital," she told us.

"Is she sick?"

"No she's not sick but Isa was rushed to the hospital in an ambulance and your mother went with her."

This was unusual nobody ever went to the doctor or the hospital unless someone had a contagious disease or they were near death. Everybody was treated at home, the doctor came with his little black bag and Mum got out our only good towel for him. We recovered at home with the aid of our family, nobody had a phone and the only way to summon an ambulance was at the police callbox at the end of our street.

We found a clean place to sit on the steps and waited impatiently for our Mum, it seems as though we spend half of our young lives sitting on the outside steps or hiding in the coal bunker when trouble was brewing.

Eventually, she turned up without Isa because she had been admitted to the hospital.

"What's wrong?" we chorused.

"You're too young to understand," said Mum as she hurried past us.

This war had caused us a great gap of explanations for the things that were happening all about us.

That night because I slept in the living room I could hear my parents talking and it was sickening. I wanted to plug my ears or scream but I was a nosy girl.

"She was pregnant and she took a long knitting needle and thrust it into her to abort the baby," Mum whispered.

"My God!" said Dad.

"She's lucky I was home her mother had gone shopping."

"Will she be okay?" Dad asked.

"Probably, but it's doubtful if she'll ever have children," said Mum sadly.

"Usually when girls get in trouble they're sent to stay with an aunt or someone in another town. Poor Isa chose the hard way to solve her problem," said Dad.

"That's true girls can't afford to make a mistake like that. Thank God our Grace is too young to get mixed up in the craziness that's going on," said Mum with a deep sigh.

I lay in bed pretending to sleep I was too young to understand because I believed most babies were wanted and nobody in their right mind would stick a needle through one. Trouble! How much trouble could a baby create for poor Isa?

This war had another victim and Isa was a ghost of her usual self, she passed us on the stairs never speaking or smiling. Her engagement to the handsome British Naval Officer was broken and in time she did go south to England to avoid the gossiping neighbors.

CHAPTER EIGHT

We had a beautiful wrought iron gate at our house and I loved to swing on it. It was decorated with leaves and flowers I traced my fingers around the patterns and dreamed of one day having paints to create beautiful artwork. When it rained I licked the raindrops with my tongue as they dripped from the patterns; unfortunately, our beautiful gate was also a victim of the war.

One day workmen drove up our street in a truck carrying welding masks and blow torches. We watched fascinated as their torches roared with a white and blue flame as they proceeded to melt the iron gates and threw them into their truck bed.

Mrs. Willis, our official street tattletale, was watching from her window, she had a beautiful garden and prided herself on her roses. Mrs. Willis had no kids; so, she didn't have to dig up her grass and plant a large Victory Garden. Every wrong movement in our street by the kids was reported to our mothers, if we picked a leaf off her hedge she became frantic; so, just for the Hell of it, we crawled along on our hands and knees when we passed her house and chugged at her hedge and left the leaves for her to find.

Suddenly, Mrs. Willis realized what the workmen were about to do when they approached her ornate gate, her door flew open and she bounded down her stairs.

"Don't you touch my property?" she demanded.

"We've been told to remove all gates and fences," said the weary workmen.

"What! You can't take my gate or fence I won't let you. I paid for this gate and it's my property."

Like Joan of Arc the poor tormented woman draped her body across her gate ready to brave the torches.

"I'm sorry you have no choice we need them for the war," said the now serious workman as he gently removed the screaming woman from her perch on top of her gate.

"Don't be ridiculous! What are they going do with them?" Mrs. Willis knew that they were determined to take her property.

"I don't know lady maybe they're going to make tanks or trucks out of the iron," he said seriously.

This time Mrs. Willis lost her battle as she kicked and fought the workers. Tiny little black stumps of iron were all that remained of the lovely handiwork.

The only gate the workmen were instructed not to remove was the huge gate to the cemetery and the dead couldn't even see it. I certainly couldn't swing on that monster it was twenty feet high with jagged points at the top.

Months later we rode past on the bus and saw all the gates and fences lying in a scrap yard rusting in the rain. Poor Mrs. Willis we hoped she didn't see them.

It seemed as though everything revolved around the war. My brothers played daily at soldiers and marched around singing stupid ditties.

"Hitler he's only got one ball/
Goring's got two but they're too small/
Himmler he's something similar/
But poor old Goebel's got no balls at all."

Lucky Hitler had a ball to play with my brothers kicked at rolled up rags or newspapers tied into the shape of a ball. John was in trouble again because he went looking for balls on the school roof, someone had told him that there was a bunch of tennis balls up there and he and his friend had climbed up the drainpipe to get them. The police brought him home with a stern warning that if he misbehaved again they would have to put him in a detention home.

That night Dad cleared the living room furniture to the sides of the room and gave him a whipping. Nobody in our family would disgrace my parents and bring the police to our door.

Poor John was prepared to run away and I found him later on the embankment overlooking the burn.

"Don't leave John," I begged.

"I'm going to run away and work on a farm, they're looking for people to work on the farms they're called the Land Army."

"You're too young and they don't hire boys they take young women," I told him.

"Well I'll stick it out a while longer, but I'm going to leave one day and probably go to New Zealand and work on a sheep farm," he sounded determined.

We walked home together and I was grateful he didn't leave I couldn't have survived without him.

John was great at building kites and inventing toys. He found tin cans, punched holes in the sides and threaded string through the holes to make stilts. The idea was that we grabbed the string and stood on the cans and stomped along. We played kick the can with a battered bean can. It was great fun! Mum gave me an old piece of clothesline for a jump rope and I skipped and sang some of the new songs that we had invented since the war began.

"Tramp, Tramp, Tramp the boys are marching/

Who's that knocking at my door?

If it's Hitler and his wife we will stab them with a knife/

And we won't see old Hitler anymore."

The name Hitler terrified me, at night I had nightmares and during the day I refused to answer the doorbell, I was convinced that the German's would eventually get me. If the German's ever crossed the English Channel I was sure they would find and kill me and, since the channel was close to England, I comforted myself with the sure knowledge that they would get the English first. My poor English cousins would all be victims to the ugly man with the cookie duster mustache.

We listened to Winston Churchill talking on the radio and it didn't sound as though this war would ever end. Ever since Uncle Johnny died Dad couldn't stand Winston Churchill he called him a warmonger. When we went to the pictures they showed the newsreels and I watched the chubby little man, obviously not on food rationing, wearing his black bowler hat and sucking on his fat cigar. He didn't look like a man who enjoyed war he had a worried look except when he met the troops then he put on his smiley face.

The King and Queen were bombed in Buckingham Palace and came out to visit the Londoner's to show them solidarity. She looked very pretty and didn't look as though she was suffering too much from rationing her clothes looked quite new; although, it was reported that they were doing whatever they could for the war effort; after all, we could hardly expect them to peel potatoes for the troops wearing their pristine white gloves. We loved the Queen Mother because she was born in Scotland.

The royal family had dogs they were corgis and I begged Mum for a pet.

"Can I have a dog?" I asked.

"No, we've barely got enough food for ourselves."

A young boy was now living with Mrs. White nobody knew if he was her grandson or an orphan, he was about my age and had a vicious temper; so, I seldom played with him. I tried once and he hit me over the head with a tennis racquet. It was rumored that he is the son of a patient from the mental hospital. He brought his plump pet cat with him and she gave birth to a litter of kittens.

One day I found him sitting by the gooseberry bushes stroking the kittens.

"Can I have one?" I pleaded.

"No," he said. "I'm going to kill them."

"What did you say?" I wasn't sure if I understood him.

"Mrs. White said I can't keep them there's too many to feed and she didn't say I could give them away. Maybe I'll drown them in the bathtub or I'll just choke them one at a time. I like to kill, it'll be easy just like wringing a chicken's neck," he said coldly.

He picked up a little black and white one and started to twist its neck, he twisted and squeezed until the little thing quit wiggling and lay dead. The mother cat stood there and was howling.

"No!" I screamed.

"Shut up, don't be a baby!"

I grabbed a black one and ran, at least one would survive I'd take this soft little kitten home and hide it in the coal bunker. He was perfect for the coal bunker he'd be invisible there.

Hiding a kitten, feeding it and keeping it warm proved to be too difficult for me and soon Mum found me sneaking off with scraps of food.

"Where did you get it?" Mum asked, as she picked up the dirty kitten.

I told her the story and she was aghast.

"Good God! That's the last time you play with that boy."

I got to keep the kitten and we named him Tito after a war hero in the Yugoslavian army he was a great cat and lived outside and roamed the garden killing mice for his food; unfortunately, he also liked to kill birds and I had to shoo him away when I saw him stalking the birds in my Little Bit of Bread and No Cheese tree.

Three brothers: John in the middle

Grace's High School Photo

Mum and Dad on their tandem bicycle

Grace: Age 16 years

"Matt and Grace at the Skating Rink"

CHAPTER NINE

Christmas came but there would be no presents for us. The English celebrate Christmas and the Scots always celebrate the New Year. Mum, being English, still believed in Christmas, but Dad had made it clear that there would be no Santa Claus coming to our house. He lectured us on self reliance and not to expect hand outs from anybody. Halloween was frowned upon my father considered it begging. We were to do our chores willingly without praise. Being conceited was not tolerated. Humility was considered a virtue. We were given pocket money and expected to save it, we were all saving for bicycles. John was the first to buy his bike because he ran errands for every housewife on our street it was a "Star".

Christmas was not celebrated in Scotland and at one time a man could be punished for not working on Christmas Day. The Scots were heard to mutter that it was just another day and, over the years, the Presbyterians acknowledged it but did not celebrate Christmas. They believed that Jesus was the son of God but they did not spend money on gifts to celebrate December 25th, a child could perhaps get a sixpence or an orange. Queen Victoria in 1870 introduced the Christmas tree to the English but it took almost another one hundred years before the Scottish began to accept the tree as one of the symbols of Christmas. The Thomson family never had a Christmas tree but on Christmas Eve we hung up our carefully darned socks and hoped for the best. John hung up a pillowcase. Mum had managed to scrounge Seville oranges and nuts and Aunt Susie had given us a jig saw puzzle. Aunt Susie, my Dad's sister, had no kids and was super with me she tried unsuccessfully to curl my short hair with a hot poker when it grew back after my encountered with the cooties. A hot poker "curl" was not one of my favorite hairstyle it scared the living daylights out of me. Aunt Susie thrust the poker into the fire and when it emerged suitably "hot" she twisted my hair around the poker. The smell of burning hair was not at all comforting. When I screamed with fright she decided to give me a rag curl which did not entail heat. Old rags were torn in strips and my wet hair was wrapped around them. Next morning the rags were removed and miraculously I was Shirley Temple.

Christmas morning we bounded out of our beds and set up the puzzle on the living room table, it was a map of the world and all the pink pieces were the British Empire. Throughout Christmas day, we built the puzzle and when we had fit every piece in we discovered one piece missing, we searched the floor but it was nowhere to be found. In walked Mum and placed the missing piece into the puzzle. I guess she wanted to fit in the last piece. We played cards in the evenings after our homework was done and especially loved Old Maid or Snap, a battle always ensued until someone was in tears. A game was never fun for me I was always given the green marker for Snakes and Ladders because green was considered an unlucky color. I dare not say I didn't want to play and had to have a stiff upper lip when I was soundly beaten.

Hogmanay (Hog-ma-nay) is the Scottish New Year and some of the Scots celebrate it by getting roaring drunk. Mum had bartered with Mrs. White and had all the ingredients to make a clootie dumpling. The word clootie means cloth in the Scottish dialect. We loved the clootie dumpling because when Mum was mixing it she always let us give it a stir and make a wish. Silver sixpences wrapped in foil were hidden for us to find. Often a child was known to choke on a hidden coin. A clootie dumpling is equivalent to an English plum pudding except the Scottish boil their dumpling wrapped in approximately a twenty-four inch square piece of cotton, usually an old pillow case, tie the cloth securely in a tight knot and plunge it into boiling water. I guess the Scots at one time were too poor to own a pudding bowl. The dumpling, once cooked, has a thick skin and on New Year's Day we slice it and when it's cold we fry it like a steak. Our rations did not extend to extra butter to make shortcake another favorite of the Scots at Hogmanay. At the stroke of midnight on New Year's Eve we were all given a glass of Mum's bramble wine and we would clink our glasses together and wished one another Happy New Year. Some people sing Auld Lang Syne. I never knew what syne meant I knew auld in the Scottish dialect meant old and lang meant long, but syne was a mystery. Our Highland teacher said it meant since, but that didn't make much sense to me. Another teacher said it meant sigh that seemed better. An old long sigh seemed more like the

Scots who were more likely to see the glass half empty than half full. For the English singers it means "Days Gone By". After midnight, we expected first footers they rang the bell and usually brought a lump of coal. I preferred a fruit cake but during the war they were nonexistent. It is important that the first foot be a man with black hair to bring the family good luck. When the first footer comes inside he presents the housewife with the coal and says, "Lang may your lum reek" it means they wish for the home warmth and prosperity. Dad had red hair so he could not be a first footer.

The best surprise during the war was one that came from Dad. At Hogmanay, he presented us with a gigantic box of Cadbury's Milk Tray Chocolates. Heavenly! The reason we had the chocolates was because Dad always read the newspaper from end to end looking for news of the war. One day he noticed an advertisement from Cadbury's the chocolate company depicting a young woman working a lathe. Women were being used in the workforce because the men were fighting and she was working on the wrong side of the machine; so, he decided to write to them to point out the error. The Cadbury Company wrote back thanking him and sent a gift of chocolates. We were allowed to eat all the toffee and nuts and Mum ate the soft centers because she was losing her teeth. Poor Mum had pyorrhea of the gums and her teeth wobbled like loose tombstones she; eventually, had to have all her teeth extracted and had to wear a false plate. We had no toothpaste or brushes and we were encouraged by Dad to rub our teeth clean with our fingers and a dab of baking soda.

Renfrewshire had school dentists and every child was required to visit them at least once a year. It was a day we dreaded! The dentist was located in downtown Greenock in the badly bombed out part of the town. The torture chamber was on the top floor of an old tenement building and to reach the dentist's office we had to climb up a stairway covered with the blood spat out by the poor kids who had teeth extracted. Teeth were rarely filled unless they were second teeth but any first teeth with decay were quickly removed. We were lucky and had inherited strong straight teeth. I believe the fact that sweets were rationed until the early 1950's probably saved hundreds of kids from bad teeth.

Our bad teeth were the least of our problems kids were getting sick and vanished from school sometimes for weeks or months. My brothers and I caught every childhood ailment including mumps, whooping cough and measles. We knew to be very careful not to step on rusty nails sticking out from the wood and debris left over from the bombings, Mum explained that we could die of tetanus or, as it's more commonly known as lock jaw, we had never had any injections to prevent any of the diseases so it's bad or good luck. Our neighbors and cousin were unlucky and caught tuberculosis. I heard that if you caught TB you would probably go to a sanitarium in Switzerland, that sounded like a good deal to me, maybe I could meet Heidi and we could climb the mountains together and see the cows with bells jingle jangling as they stomped around the meadows. Scottish Belted Galloway's were not musical they were more interested in chewing the cud than bell ringing.

"Can I go visit cousin Ian?" I asked.

"Definitely not, you know he has TB," replied Mum.

"I'll just sit by his door and read to him."

"I told you no! You know that TB is deadly!" Mum yelled.

My friend May Balentine had TB and was absent from school; so, without my Mum's permission I decided to visit her. May, was an only child and had lovely dolls and books that had once belonged to her mother when she was young.

"Can I play with May?" I asked her mother.

"Sure come on in."

Obviously, her mother didn't have any qualms about visitors catching TB.

There sat May propped up in bed with lots of pillows, she didn't even look sick unless you count a wicked cough as sick. She had books, dolls and games strewn all over her bed. Fantastic!

I played with her for the rest of the day and went home expecting to start coughing and spitting up blood any minute, it didn't happen; so, I figured I'd never go to Switzerland to visit Heidi and hear the cow bells ringing or hear my voice echoing back to me as I yodeled in the Alps.

CHAPTER TEN

Summer came and we went on picnics with Mum and Aunt Betty, she visited us from England and lived in Morden, Surrey. Aunt Betty was probably my Mum's favorite sister; unfortunately, Mum didn't like Uncle Joe who, as she liked to put it, had a hollow leg filled with cheap Irish whiskey. He was an Irishman and loved his pint and a half, Mum said he could drink the British Isles dry of whiskey and was pickled. I never noticed the smell of vinegar from him but he did smell of beer. He worked at the hospital in the morgue and many of the families put coins in the deceased eyes to pay their way into Heaven, Uncle Joe removed the silver and put a penny instead. Joe said, Saint Peter would notice a distinct drop in his revenue at the pearly gate when he worked in the morgue. He was a skinny little man and laughed with sheer delight when he told us stories. The Irish have a great way with the blarney. When we visited Joe in England he always came home falling down drunk; so, Mum decided to teach him a lesson by opening all the windows in his bedroom, throwing back his blankets and hoping he'd die of hypothermia. Joe awoke next morning rosy cheeked, very healthy and gobbled down a huge breakfast.

When Aunt Betty visited us we always went to Spango Valley to collect hazelnuts, this was before IBM built there and wiped out the hazelnut trees. The nuts were a valuable source of food for us. The kids always went to the woods and the grownups sat in the meadow and enjoyed the sun while we played hide and seek. I'm not keen on the woods I hate creepy crawly insects that might bite me I usually sat on the path and waited for the boys.

I was crouching on the path and playing with a long stick and splashing it into a puddle. I saw him coming he was a tall man with dirty blond hair, thin horn rimmed glasses and a rain coat was draped over his arm. He walked carefully around a puddle and stood above me.

"Are you alone?" he asked.

"No."

"I don't see anybody, where are they?" The stranger asked as he looked around him.

"My big brothers are playing in the woods," I said looking up at him.

"Are you cold, I can give you my coat to keep you warm?"

He took his coat and began to wrap it around my shoulders as it dipped into the muddy puddle.

Mum had warned us about strangers but this man seemed nice and friendly; so, I wasn't afraid when he bent across to pick me up and suddenly I heard Duncan's voice.

"What the Hell are you doing with my sister?"

The stranger looked startled, grabbed his coat and took off at a gallop along the path and out of sight.

Duncan gently guided me back to Mum who immediately went ballistic and ran off into the woods to find the "dirty bugger". I'm almost glad she didn't catch him because she would have been jailed for murder. I sat and wondered what the big fuss was about a man offering to keep me warm seemed harmless and nobody had explained the danger I was in. I was left to puzzle over why this seemingly "nice" man was a dirty bugger. All the way home from the picnic that day we were lectured about not trusting.

My brothers resented having to look after me every day and took pains to find ways to keep me out of trouble. On weekends they liked to go fishing with a stick, string and a bent safety pin. I helped them find worms in the garden and we went to the Greenock pier to fish. The pier had stout posts and we sat there for hours fishing. The boys could swim and, to protect me, they took a length of rope and tied me to one of the posts in case I fell into the deep water. I loved those days and after fishing we walked along the shoreline and searched the rocks for shells. Mum would never allow us to eat shellfish she considered them dirty but we could see lots of poor tinkers and homeless families boiling rusty cans filled with water and cooking the whelks. I was offered the dead snail-like whelk many times but as hungry as I was I could never bring myself to eat them. The shoreline was covered with oil from the many ships that sailed up the River Clyde. My brothers usually caught fish that, in better days, would have been thrown back but we were hungry; so, we took them home to be fried with chips made from the potatoes grown in our garden. I never told Mum how I spent my days fishing tied up to a post. Tattle tales were not tolerated.

That September John went to the Mount School; so I was left on my own in the primary school. The Mount School for boys was probably the toughest school for miles around, many of the boys there came from impoverished homes and knew no boundaries. Some; unfortunately, had trouble with the law and ended up in a borstal for delinquents. That night, when John came home he was covered with welts and bruises.

"Well I hope the other boy looks half as bad as you," said Mum. "What happened?"

"It's the gauntlet. I had to run through a line of boys and they all punched or kicked me. It's an initiation a sort of welcome to the school," explained John.

"My God!" gasped Mum. "I don't remember your brothers coming home in that state."

"Oh sure they did everybody goes through it," John bragged.

"Look at your trousers," Mum gasped.

Once again, John had ripped pants this time they were knee less.

"Maybe I should go up to the Mount and see the Headmaster."

"No Mum, don't do that I'll never live it down, and they'll beat me even more," begged John.

John no longer played with me he was a teenager now and ran wild with the other boys after school. I had found a new friend her name was Irene she had several brothers and sisters and was having a rough time since her father died.

"Did your dad die in the war?" I asked.

"No," she said. "He drowned in a puddle."

"Drowned in a puddle that's impossible!" This, I thought, must be a lie.

"You can if you're drunk and the puddle is deep," Irene said sadly.

Irene's father was a cooper and made the barrels for the whiskey; unfortunately he drank more than his share of spirits and his "spirit" soon departed. Without a father this was another family, because of alcohol, doomed to a life of poverty.

Drunken fathers were the worst curse a family could have, I was grateful that my father hated the stuff and impressed on us the evils of alcoholism; however, Dad did smoke Capstan cigarettes and sometimes he smoked a pipe, Mum hated it and nagged him constantly to quit, he said it calmed his nerves and, when the war was over, he'd quit and buy a tandem and we'd all go touring the youth hostels together.

We believed the war would soon be over because the allies were giving the German's a run for their money. When we watched the Pathe news at the pictures we saw the German's surrender. Hitler now, in the newsreels, doesn't look so pompous he is a shell of his former self and his army was recruiting boys to fight for the Fatherland. He had those wee boys goose stepping in parades wearing fine leather boots and barely able to shoulder a gun. Lucky boys my Mum couldn't buy us shoes for love nor money!

I wished the rationing would end because it was getting harder to stomach the food Mum had to serve us, she was now dishing up tripe and it richly deserves its name. Mum served it with onions which are my least favorite vegetable. Tripe is offal and should only be served to animals in the zoo. Animals eat the entrails of beasts and during the war this is what we were reduced to eating. I had no idea where the good meat was being served but it certainly wasn't being dished up in Scotland. A hungry child for a parent is difficult to bear, a caring mother can suffer almost anything for her children but to know that they are hungry and she can't feed them good food is the worst kind of pain.

"Yuck! I can't eat this muck," I complained.

"Eat it or you'll go to bed hungry," said my poor exhausted mother, she had lined up that morning and accepted what was available at the butchers.

I shoved the food as quickly as I could into my mouth, ran to the toilet and threw it up. Refusing to eat a meal at our house was never tolerated and we swallowed and gulped whatever was served. Mealtimes were Hell as we sat in abject terror never knowing when we would be thumped for eating too fast or too slow, talking too much, elbows on the table were swiped off along with the plate of food, and to leave the table without being excused meant we wouldn't be allowed to eat at the next meal. If we complained that somebody got a bigger portion then a knife would appear and your piece would be cut in half.

I hated black pudding it looked like chunks of dog shit on my plate it is made mainly of very little meat, animal blood, spices and bread. My favorite meal was fish and chips but every time I ate chips I felt sick because the lard was kept unrefrigerated on the stove for months and was obviously alive with bacteria.

By the war's end we were reduced to eating from tin cups and plates, for water we drank from jelly jars. One of John's jobs was to clear the table and to carry the dirty dishes to the sink; unfortunately, being careful was never one of his strong points and he dropped and broke every dish and the stores had no china to sell.

"We're like tinkers," complained Mum. "I'll have to see if my sister has any spare plates or cups."

"If that's the only thing we have to complain about in this war we're a lucky bunch."

Dad was always the one to bring us back to reality.

CHAPTER ELEVEN

Approximately, a year after D-Day June 6th, 1944, when the allies landed in Europe to free the people from the Nazis the war was over thanks mainly to the USA for joining us in the fight against Hitler. Poor Britain was on its last legs and probably couldn't have lasted much longer. VE Day was the happiest day of my young life no longer did we have to dread the dark and the bombers dropping their deadly cargo. We were to have a bonfire at the bottom of our street and roast spuds, the kids were given the job of collecting wood, paper and anything that would burn. Unknown to Mrs. Willis, the boys had carried off her old garden bench and heaved it onto the fire, poor Mrs. Willis she tried so hard to keep her garden a special place.

Mum tore up old sheets to make flags of all the countries that participated in winning the war, she was busy plunging the threadbare sheets up and down in the boiler and dyeing them various colors, I think the first strong wind and they'll all be in tatters. I helped her sew the Red Ensign for Canada, the Stars and Stripes for the USA and as many flags as we could. Fireworks were supplied for the celebration and the adults were having a dance. At long last we could all breathe a collective sigh of relief. I am overjoyed that I will not have to learn German!

On Saturdays we went by train to Glasgow to the picture show. The station still had the posters warning us to be careful that the enemy may be listening. We caught the LMS steam engine train at the West Station and every time the soot would blow into my eye, Dad would lick the corner of his handkerchief roll up my upper lid or pull down the lower lid of my eye and extract the black soot. The trains were old clunkers and we rode third class smokers because Dad was still trying to quit smoking. The carriages were dirty and the seats covered in soot because passengers who didn't smoke and, were gasping for fresh air, foolishly opened the windows and allowed the soot to blow inside. In Glasgow Mum shopped for whatever little food there was available and Dad and I tagged along. Mum always shopped at Lewis' but my favorite shop in Glasgow was H. Samuels the jewelers, they had a window display and one particular item that I adored was a Royal Dalton Figurine dressed in a colorful crinoline dress. I had never had a doll and now I was too old for them but I promised myself that one day I would own one of those beautiful ladies. After shopping we went to the picture show which usually ended up with Dad leaving his seat if the Pathe News showed anything to do with the war. Poor Dad he still can't get over Uncle Johnny's death; unfortunately, the news was worse than ever, a British detachment exposed Belsen Concentration Camp in the vicinity of Hanover, Germany and found typhus raging, forty thousand sick and starving people and thirteen thousand dead people stacked on the ground. Skeletons piled like bundles of wood and the living dressed in rags, wide eyed and staggering about on stick like legs begging for food. Mum was never troubled by horror, death or murder her favorite reading was True Detective stories and she bragged that she could probably commit the perfect crime because she religiously read about so many murders. After the war Mum had read that one of the commandants of the many concentration camps had used tattooed skin for lamp shades and this was described in detail in one of her gory books. On the other hand Dad had no stomach for the miseries of life depicted at the movies and he escaped to the foyer. It seemed that the Nazis were worse than we suspected and exterminated thousands of innocent people and, according to the commentator they had been forced into a gas chamber by guards and snarling dogs. We were extremely grateful that they had lost the war; usually, the journey home from Glasgow was tortuous because by then Mum had fallen out with Dad over some trivial misunderstanding. We walked home from the West Station in stony silence and as we passed the street gaslights, now lit for the first time since the war ended, I asked my parents about the horrors we had seen on the news.

"Why did Hitler kill so many families? Was it because they were Jews?"

Silence!

"What is a Jew?" I asked.

"Jewish people are called Jews because it's a religion just like a Catholic or a Presbyterian," explained Dad.

"So Hitler killed all those people because of their religion?" I asked

"Hitler was brought up, either by his parents or church, to believe Jews were bad," he explained.

"We have Bible studies every day and I've never ever heard the teacher say bad things about Jews. Why did he kill little kids?"

"Grace, you're too young to understand a person like Hitler. It's just like war, nobody in their right mind wants a war but leaders disagree and people die," said my Dad.

I dropped the subject knowing that to discuss it further would be painful to my parents but I knew it would take a great deal of explanation to convince me that killing thousands of innocent people would solve anything.

That night as we wearily walked home by gaslight and, as I watched my shadow appear and disappear, I began to think of those little kids being led to a gas chamber I wanted to cry out the words of a hymn," Jesus loves the little children." Instead I asked,

"Dad, Jesus was a Jew and they crucified him. Do you think Jewish people have a tough time in this world?"

Dad looked down at me and quietly said," Good question."

My question was never answered by Dad and the gaps in my education were enormous.

CHAPTER TWELVE

Uncle Jock came home from the Merchant Navy and within a very short time his wife Aunt Bunny was expecting a baby, it seemed that every second female in the street was expecting. The expected babies were called baby boomers.

Aunt Bunny gave birth to twin girls and six weeks later she died. The cause of her death was a massive infection caused by unsanitary conditions. Mum called it White Leg and said it was a common cause of death and, as I looked at my poor auntie in her coffin I imagined her to have a pure white leg. Uncle Jock was devastated and sat staring into the fire he now had six children to raise.

Granny came back from England with my Mum's sisters for the funeral and I went with my Mum and Dad to meet them. I loved my aunties they were a chubby happy group of women so very different from my Mum. Mum was the skinny one of the family and seemed never to sit at ease. It was my first funeral and the saddest. A young

78

husband surviving the war only to return home and nine months later his young wife is dead. Dad went home after the funeral and I sat with Mum quietly listening to Granny and her daughters.

"What is he going to do?" Aunt Betty asked.

"Well I can take one of the twin babies," offered Aunt Bella.

"I can take the other," said Aunt Bunny's sister.

"I can take care of the four older kids," said Granny. Granny was seventy years old and this would be a difficult task because my cousins had been running wild for months and paid little or no attention to adults.

Mum looked at her brother Jock and asked.

"Is this what you want?"

"No, I don't want my twin girls to grow up apart," he replied

"Well in that case I'll take care of the twin babies," said my Mum.

I helped her dress the lovely twins and loaded them into a gigantic pram and we started the walk home. They had no clothes just one or two nightgowns but I felt sure my Mum would soon rectify this with her busy fingers and sewing machine.

"What's Dad going to say if we bring home the twin girls?" I asked

"Nothing, he'll accept my decision."

Of course she was right and when we reached our front door Dad swung it open welcoming us home, he never ever opposed her it just wasn't wise.

"I expected this," he said

The house was changed completely with the addition of the two babies, nappies drying by the fire, bottles being washed and refilled, taking turns to feed them when they could eat solid food and best of all playing with them, at last I had two live dolls. Our family walked on tip toe when Jenny and Mary slept but when they were awake we reveled in their every smile. Love is the greatest gift of all and we loved those babies and Mum seemed to regain her joy and was no longer quick to slap us for every little misdeed.

When they were two years old the baby girls started to call my parents Mum and Dad so it was time to approach Uncle Jock to arrange a more permanent solution. I went with them to see Granny and to talk to Uncle Jock.

"Jock, we'd like to adopt the twins," said Mum.

No reply. He had a reputation of being a sullen fellow and rarely spoke.

"We need to draw up papers of adoption we can't keep the kids indefinitely they think Davie and I are their parents," explained Mum.

"No I want my kids back," he said.

"Who'll take good care of them? You don't expect our mother to look after six kids," Mum replied.

"I'll send someone to collect my daughters," said Jock.

"This is ridiculous you'll kill our mother she's seventy-two!" Mum yelled.

Granny sat there quietly clasping her hands and rolling her thumbs back and forth. Mum knew it was a losing battle Granny always gave into her youngest and only son.

Next day a neighbor girl arrived at our house to collect the babies. Mum dressed them in the clothes she had lovingly made and cried as she buttoned their tiny dresses.

I believe my Mum never recovered from the loss and every time she went to see the babies she came home more depressed. The twin girls were dirty and neglected. Granny was having a difficult time and her son was oblivious to his mother's distress.

Shortly after the babies left Aunt Liz came to stay with us with her baby girl. Aunt Liz was my father's sister and her husband was another drunken Scotsman who vanished one day, it was rumored he was in jail. Mum was in a poor state of mind and watching Aunt Liz with her baby did not offer her any comfort after losing the twin babies. One night we were awakened by Mum rummaging through the tool shed.

"What on earth are you doing Gracie?" asked Dad.

"I'm going to the cemetery to dig my own grave."

"What!" Dad yelled, he thought she was sleepwalking.

"You heard me I'm going to dig my own grave," she said as though in a daze.

"Come back to bed, we'll talk about this in the morning."

This was the first of many strange incidents when our mother threatened suicide we lived in dread and never knew when she would go off half cocked. Mum had lived through two wars, the depression, bombings, rationing, and now it appeared she was beginning to crack.

Aunt Liz moved out and placed her daughter in an orphanage and obtained a job there to be close to her baby. It was impossible to live in the Thomson home.

Shortly after the babies left we were offered a new house with a bedroom for me. I was overjoyed but it was probably one of the worst moves our parents made. The house was in a district called Larkfield and it was one in a row of four, this meant we had to access our backdoor by walking around the outside path of our neighbor's house. Within a very short time of moving Mum quarreled with our neighbor, she sieved every conversation looking for insults or any small gesture and pounced on the offender. She hated the house because it was built beside a steep hill and the smoke backfired into the living room every time

the fire was lit. Our house definitely was in the category of
"lang may your lum reek".

I bought my bike that year it was a Phillips and was as
heavy as a tank. Now that we all have bikes the family goes
on cycling holidays. Mum rides a tandem with Dad because
she never learned to ride a bike. We sailed to Ireland to
tour the north and I met my Dad's Uncle Sam Gibson his
father's brother and; thereby, I discovered my grandfather's
history. I had thought that he had fled from Ireland because
he was a member of the IRA, it turned out he escaped
to Scotland and left an insane wife and a bad marriage.
Divorces were almost unheard of so he presented himself to
my grandmother as a single man; eventually, he married my
grandmother after his first wife died.

The fortnight we toured Northern Ireland it rained every
day; consequently, I saw Ireland from the uncomfortable
seat of a bike with the rain pouring down my face. My
impressions of this beautiful country were that the country
roads were bad, it rains too much, and the countryside is
green, the people are friendly, kind and have a subtle sense
of humor; also, just like Scotland, Ireland has more than its
share of pubs. The Irish have long memories and are like
the elephants they never forget an injustice; unfortunately,
my Mum was unable to shop in some stores there because
of her English accent, the Irish have a long history of hatred
towards the English. We stayed in Youth Hostels and boy
were they primitive! The beds were wooden framed canvas
hammocks and in some cases were stacked in four levels.
Like a fool, I chose the top and had to climb down over
three sleeping bodies to go to the bathroom. Bathroom,
what a misnomer, there wasn't a bathroom just a dry toilet at
the backside of the hostel, this awful three-holed outhouse
stunk worse than a pigpen.

One day in Dublin we were posed on a bridge so that Dad could take some photographs and a wee Irishman, strolling along with his dog, approached us and stopped. He took a long look at Dad and said,

"Sure now laddie you're too old for short pants, you need to tell your Ma that you're ready for long trousers."

Dad always wore shorts when he cycled and the funny little man, with a twinkle in his eye, thought he was too old for them.

Every year we toured the British Isles for our summer holidays. Weather is the deciding factor for bike riding, if it rained we were drenched and unable to dry our clothes at the hostels, when it was hot we burned and found it impossible to sleep on uncomfortable beds with red hot skin. I would have loved to have gone to the seaside and relax but instead I was forced to carry loaded pannier bags filled with canned goods and to picnic in the woods with horse flies eating me and my meal. A holiday, what a joke, every year I dreaded when July came around and I had to take part in the endurance test. Being brought up the hard way was damned hard!

CHAPTER THIRTEEN

I passed the qualifying exam and started high school. The high school was a bus ride away and it meant I was leaving earlier in the morning and returning later at night. I had to be sure that I never missed the bus because if I did Mum would wait for me at the bus stop and beat me all the way home. I was repeatedly slapped on my head to knock some sense into my thick skull; unfortunately, after repeated slaps my ear drums were punctured. The beatings were something I came to accept but it was humiliating to be slapped in front of friends. This is a sure way to bring up a resentful child or to raise one with absolutely no confidence, and yet I loved my Mum with all her miserable ways she was the hub of our home and kept the wheels turning.

Dad was now working at the Royal Naval Torpedo Factory, Alexandria, Dunbartonshire and the factory was on the other side of the River Clyde. He left at five a.m.

and did not return until very late. My three brothers were apprentice joiners at the shipyards and upon completion of their apprenticeship the twins would be entering the armed forces. A joiner is not a carpenter, the joiner makes beautiful furniture and they are responsible for the fine woodwork in the Captain's cabin. The joiners work is finished by a French polisher and several coats of stain are applied until the piece of work shines.

Mum continued to visit Granny and to help her with Jock's large family because Granny's health was rapidly declining.

One day my cousin came to see my mother to ask for help.

"Aunt Grace I'm being annoyed by my Dad," complained Margaret

"What do you mean annoyed?" replied Mum.

"Well he's coming into my bedroom and annoying me. I need you to talk to him," cried Margaret.

I sat and listened to see what my Mum's reaction would be to my cousin's plea for help.

"I don't believe you, my brother Jock would never do a thing like that!" she protested.

"You're wrong, he did."

"I don't want to talk about this again and that's the subject closed," Mum stomped out of the room banging the door behind her.

"I hate him," sobbed Margaret.

That day I knew how my cousin felt, it's easy to hate someone you love after they disappoint you it's hard to believe that someone you trust could completely destroy your faith in people for years to come. I had suffered a similar problem, not with my father, but with my twin brothers. The incidents happened in the dead of night, they chose their small sister to learn the female anatomy. My instinct told me to complain, but in the Thomson household it was useless to blame Mum's beloved twins. I was ten years old when this happened, they were eighteen. I solved the problem by jamming a chair against my bedroom door.

Shortly after my cousin came to see us Granny became very ill and my Mum and I went to visit her, she was lying in bed groaning.

"What's wrong mother, have you seen a doctor?" asked Mum.

"No, my stomach feels awful."

The doctor arrived and diagnosed Granny with senile decay, probably cancer, and said she would have to be hospitalized.

My dear Granny was taken to the asylum, the only hospital with a bed available, and died that night surrounded by the mentally ill patients. Mum had refused to care for her.

Once again my aunties came from England, this time for their mother's funeral it was to take place at our house. I was given the job of going for all the wreaths at the florist I ordered five wreaths. The florist was so overjoyed with such a big order he gave me a free bag of fruit. I munched all the way home.

The flowers arrived the next day along with Granny in her coffin.

"Where will we put her?" asked Dad.

"Put her in Grace's room."

"What!" I gasped. "I don't want a dead body in my room."

"Don't be stupid your Granny wouldn't hurt you when she was alive so why would she bother you when she's dead? Besides, your room is at the end of the hallway and the undertakers don't need to turn the coffin to take it outside," explained Mum

"That's not fair," I protested. "Dead bodies sometimes smell."

"I'll spray Eau De Cologne in the room," said Mum.

Granny did not smell but the cologne stunk and I hated perfume for years to come and, as I lay in bed looking up at the open coffin sitting on a table, I could not sleep. My white faced Granny dressed in her shroud, her eyes closed and sunken cheeks gave me the creeps. I had always remembered her with a round chubby face but now her face looked so small and shriveled. I had loved this old woman all my life and this was going to be my last memory of her.

The funeral for Granny was difficult, the tears came in copious amounts but the event after the funeral provided me with another insight into greed and resentment. My Granny did not leave a large estate all her money had been used to help support my Uncle Jock and his six children but she did have some attractive pins and necklaces that my grandfather had given her when he had sailed the seven seas. The sisters divided the spoils of death and, at the end of their plunder and arguing over every bobble some were happy and others deeply resentful, I was asked if I would like anything.

"No thanks, I don't want beads but if nobody wants the tin of small sea shells I would love to string them on fishing line and make a bracelet."

This was my inheritance from my Granny and I treasured them like the finest jewels.

CHAPTER FOURTEEN

One day in high school we were asked to bring our birth certificate to our home room. My home room teacher was Miss MacDonald, a spinster from the Highlands of Scotland, who instructed us on the Bible. She called me to the front of the class and asked.

"Why doesn't your birth certificate have the date of your Christening?

"I wasn't Christened my parents didn't have the money," I explained.

"Rubbish!" she spluttered. "It doesn't cost much to have a baby christened."

"It costs more than my parents could afford," I told her.

Miss MacDonald had a pockmarked fat face, her cheeks wobbled when she spoke and spit propelled in the direction of the student. She reminded me of a walrus, coarse hair grew on her lip and out of her nose.

"Well girls, we have a heathen among us," she announced.

From that day forth Miss MacDonald made my life Hell this woman made a science out of being a bigot. We had assembly every Wednesday and Friday mornings and a girl would be chosen to read the Bible lesson, without fail she humiliated me in front of the class. If she could have tattooed a scarlet letter on my forehead she would gladly have done it, she informed the class in one of her lessons on religion that I was doomed and did not have a chance of Heaven; nevertheless, I hardened myself to her cruel words and loved the school church and especially enjoyed the hymns. My favorite hymn was "Land of our birth, we pledge to thee" which we sang with great gusto pledging our love, toil and loyalty in the years to come to Scotland. A pledge I knew I would break because I intended to leave home as soon as I could.

Shortly after this my Mum came to the school to see my art work. Miss Scott, the art teacher, had given me the highest marks for my watercolors. Mum never came to school unless we were in trouble and; unfortunately, that day she met Miss MacDonald, the assistant to the headmistress, and it was obvious Mum was born in England even though she had lived over thirty years in Scotland the English accent was still evident. To Miss MacDonald she was a "SASSENACH"! My fate was already sealed with this ugly old crone and from that day forth Miss MacDonald had another reason to torment me. I began to realize that all Christians did not exactly live up to their faith of loving one another.

We had several really excellent teachers I admired in high school I especially liked the art teacher Miss Scott, she discovered that I could draw and encouraged me to pursue my dreams of becoming a teacher. It was a dream I knew would never happen.

"We'll have no ladies in this house going to college. It's a waste of good money educating a girl. You'll go out and find a job like the rest of us," my mother informed me. Too bad my mother did not realize that if you educate a girl you educate a family. If you educate a boy you educate an individual.

Very few men in Scotland wear a kilt and those that do don't always look good in them but Mr. MacCoy our shorthand, typing and bookkeeping teacher was a hunk. He was the only male in a swarm of women and when this handsome man walked about the room with his kilt swishing back and forth it was enough to make us breathless. He had a smile for every young lassie in his class—we were all in love! To add to his charm he wore after shave lotion; whereas, the men I met stunk of body odor.

Mr. MacCoy's class was held in a small room at the end of a long dark hallway; luckily, for his pupils he kept his class well lit with lamps he had obviously brought from home. The typewriters were old Underwood and Royal wrecks and if all the keys worked we were indeed fortunate the keys were all blank; so, we had to learn to touch type. I loved typing and quickly became top in my class. Pitman's shorthand was more challenging but again I rapidly reached the required speed of 120 w.p.m. Bookkeeping was a bore and probably more suited for a girl who wanted to work in a bank. I knew this was not for me I had trouble counting two buses going past.

We had an Australian teacher her name was Miss Grey and the girls adored her. She was dynamic! She organized intra mural sports between the schools something unheard of in Greenock at that time. Most importantly, she discovered that the girls in her class could not swim and she set out to correct what she considered a necessity. The British Isles is surrounded by water and yearly kids were drowned in rivers and lochs.

She stood in front of the class her arms on her waist, this athletic blond goddess, and announced that she intended to help us overcome our fear of the water. Within weeks a school bus arrived and Miss Grey took us to the Battery Swimming Pool. The Battery Pool was close to the River Clyde and the jelly fish, crabs and seaweed floated on the water.

"Come on girls, jump in." Miss Grey's happy voice beckoned us into the water.

For warmth we clustered together a frozen group of skinny girls in our shapeless knitted swimsuits truly thankful that our school was segregated from boys. The wind blew in from the River Clyde and the water was barely fifty-five degrees, our teeth were chattering, our fingers were slowly turning blue as we dared one another to jump into the frigid water to join our eager teacher.

"Come on, it's invigorating!" called Miss Grey this lovely Australian.

Slowly we tiptoed to the edge and carefully slipped into the shallow end, our knitted suits stretched in the cold water exposing our tiny budding breasts as the neckline slid down to our waists. A comical sight! Miss Grey was right there to grasp us and to watch our desperate attempts. I gave it my best try because I was tired of being thrown into the water by my twin brothers when they reluctantly took me to the pool, they did not want a young sister tagging along they were interested in much older girls.

"Come on Grace, you can do it," Miss Grey coaxed me into the icy water.

Miss Grey was a determined woman and before the lessons ended she had several of the girls swimming back and forth across the pool. I was truly grateful that I was one of the girls who succeeded that day although my strokes were more like a dog paddle. I hated getting the water in my ears and kept my head out of the water like a pup.

Another wonderful thing Miss Grey did for us was to teach us to dance. Ballroom dancing was not encouraged only Scottish Country Dancing, we were taught The Dashing White Sergeant and reels but never the foxtrot or the waltz. Miss Grey brought records to the school and within a short time she had us waltzing and attempting to foxtrot around the gym. She played her own records of "In the Mood" and our favorite crooner Bing Crosby; unfortunately, for me I was a tall girl and had to lead. I led every partner for the rest of my life when I went dancing.

Miss Grey was quietly dismissed at the end of one year; obviously, the staid Miss MacBain, the headmistress, did not approve of her teaching methods, she would stand on the upper staircase above the gym frowning down on us like a disapproving tyrant.

Good bye Miss Grey.

Australia I thank you!

Sex was a taboo subject in the Presbyterian School and girls learned whatever they could from older sisters or from one another. I was clueless!

One day Miss MacBain summoned me to her study—I was terrified of her. This woman was the coldest female I had ever met she was like a corpse and had beaten me severely, without emotion, my first day of high school when I had made the mistake of warming my fingers on the radiator in the cloakroom.

"What are you doing?" Miss MacBain yelled.

"I'm warming my hands on the radiator Miss MacBain."

"Come with me and I'll be happy to warm your hands," she instructed.

I followed her to the study where she produced her belt. Whack! Whack! Whack! Three of her best were inflicted on my hands and wrists with the belt twisting like a snake and slapping my bare legs.

The morning I was summoned to her study I anticipated three more whacks from her belt for some unknown infraction but instead there sat my Mum. I was torn with terror either Miss MacBain was there to punish me or my mother.

"Mrs. Thomson I'll allow you to take care of your daughter," said Miss MacBain.

I was more afraid of my Mum's punishment than Miss MacBain's, I stood there transfixed. Had she borrowed MacBain's belt or was there a severe slapping in store for me? I searched my mind trying to remember what I might have done wrong before I left home that morning I always washed the breakfast dishes, made my bed, and cleaned the bathroom sink.

"What have I done?" I asked petrified.

"Did you know that you have your periods?" Mum said.

"Periods, what's that?" I asked, stepping away from her.

"Didn't you notice the blood? You're unwell and will have to wear a pad," she informed me.

"Unwell, what do you mean, I don't feel sick," I replied puzzled.

It was almost impossible to see blood on my knickers because they were dark brown. Our school uniform colors were chocolate brown and turquoise blue, colors especially picked to hide any dirt because they were seldom washed. The only bright color was the turquoise blue blouse that every girl was required to sew.

"Come with me and I'll fix you," instructed my Mum.

I was escorted into MacBain's private washroom and there, to my amazement and shock was a stain on my brown knickers. Mum pinned a pad to my underwear made of old terry cloth baby nappies and informed me I was fixed for that day.

I walked like a cowboy back to my class, the homemade pad chafing my inner thighs. I was mystified by the entire process as my Mum had failed to discuss the subject. I thought my condition was something that nobody else in my school had and should be kept a secret.

At tea time, in front of the entire family, I had my first lecture on sex and it was probably the most confusing day of my life.

"You're a woman now and if you misbehave you can become pregnant. A girl cannot afford to make any mistakes," she informed me.

Oh my God! This was the mistake they had discussed the day Isa our neighbor had gone to the hospital. Would I one day be taking a knitting needle and sticking it inside me? I still didn't understand sex and I wasn't about to get any further education from my Mum.

I stood there a miserable wretch of less than 100 pounds, a bust as flat as a twelve year old boy, being lectured by a woman who hadn't a clue how to explain menstruation to her daughter. The only thing I could feel was this wad of hard, rough cloth between my legs. I was told I had to wash this "bloody" rag every night before going to bed and to hang it out on the clothes line to dry. Every month, I washed those disgusting rags and crept out in the dark and pegged them on the clothes line. I rose at dawn to bring them inside before anyone could see them. No wonder women called it The Curse!

CHAPTER FIFTEEN

One of the happiest days for me was the day they announced on the radio that the sweeties would no longer be rationed. I had been saving my pocket money for weeks in anticipation of that day. No more coupons to clip for a miserable two ounces. It was a Sunday and I walked to the newsagent to buy the Sunday papers for my parents. Mum liked the New of the World, Dad hated that paper and called it a "rag" he preferred something more newsworthy. There was a long queue of adults at the shop and I joined them and, as I walked slowly up to the counter, until it was my turn I looked at all the sweeties that we had been deprived of throughout the war: macaroons, jelly beans, gumdrops, allsorts, coconut snowballs chocolate, etc, I salivated and decided I'd have as many as I could afford.

"I've come for my parent's papers," I told the newsagent.

He handed me the two papers and, when I hesitated to leave, he asked if there was anything else he could do for me.

"Yes sir, I'd like some sweeties. Is it true we don't need coupons anymore," I asked politely.

"That's true lass, what would you like?

I figured I had just enough money to buy at least two of my favorite sweets but I sure wished I could have them all. As I fumbled with my coins and counted them to see what I could afford I heard a man's voice from behind me saying, "Lads, let's treat this kid to as many sweeties as she wants she's been deprived long enough throughout this bloody war."

He took off his cap and passed it down the queue to the waiting men. I could hear the clink, clink, clink as the coins were tossed into the cap.

I went home that day with a bag full of sweeties to share with my family. Nobody could ever say to me that Scotsmen are stingy.

Life went on and I was increasingly miserable at home because I quickly realized that Mum had a borderline personality disorder. I was always aware that she was volatile and I had to ensure that I had a quick exit as soon as she blew her stack. The least little infraction could send her into a rage and she would chase us, catch us and thrash the living daylights out of us, Dad placated her and explained her behavior as a "change of life". This life change had been going on for a long time and I hoped when it came we would have a happier mother.

We had a dance at the end of the fourth year in high school and the boys from the Mount School were invited. Mum ordered me a dress by mail from a magazine and when it arrived I was disappointed—it was truly UGLY! I was sure that I'd be a wallflower for the entire evening. The dress was a washed out blue taffeta with coffee colored lace and a very low neckline. I had no bust and it fell open at the neck; so,

I stuffed two handkerchiefs in my bra and miraculously I had a figure. I went to the dance wearing the ugly dress and hid in a group of giggling girls. The teachers separated the girls to one side of the hall and the pimpled face boys to the other. We were given a ticket and told to seek our partner, I looked at my ticket and saw I was Josephine and I had to seek Napoleon. I made my way to the tallest boy and was disappointed; finally, I found Napoleon it was the "kitten killer", he hadn't changed much except now he had more than his share of pimples. He barely reached my shoulders he was the shortest boy in the hall.

"Hello," I said. "Do you remember me?"

No reply. He stared up at me and gulped.

"We've been partnered," I told him

The kitten killer had lost his tongue.

"I know I'm taller than you, do you have a tall friend?"

Still no answer, maybe one of the "cats" got his tongue.

"You could swop your ticket with a tall boy because I have a dainty friend for you."

Luckily, his classmate was a tall boy and he gladly exchanged tickets we had a great time; however, I did discover that boys when they held me close had a problem with their penis it became extremely hard. I asked my Mum about this and again I got no explanation. Another blank page in my sex education and I was about to enter the adult world of work and dating.

At the end of my school days I had three choices of a career a nurse, secretary or a school teacher. The latter required university and I knew that was not in the cards for me. A nurse was out because that required good math skills. That left a secretary and I would be required to attend a commercial college for one to two years.

The last day of school was a very sad day for me because as I left the final assembly at the church. I walked home with complete dread I knew my Mum would be waiting on me ready to pounce.

"Well, what are you going to do?" she asked.

I knew I wasn't ready to work I wanted to continue my education. Further education would have to be paid for and this would definitely not be offered unless I went to night school and I paid for my books, instructions and worked a part-time job. Part-time work was unavailable unless I was willing to scrub floors for the gentry. No thanks I had my share of scrubbing floors at home.

The mindset of my parents was that you did not pay to educate a female because the money would be wasted. Most women in Scotland married before they were twenty-one; so, the idea was to find a good paying job for the short time she worked and hopefully she'd be married.

"We'll have to go to the Labor Exchange to see if they have any jobs," said Mum.

The female at the Labor Exchange suggested the mill. The mill was where most of the young women ended up even if they were a dunce or a genius they were paid good wages but I refused to go there I couldn't stand the idea of a menial humdrum job. The Merino Mill processed the sheered sheep coat and manufactured beautiful sweaters, socks and almost all the woolen clothes worn throughout Scotland and exported throughout the world. Some of the jobs were extremely labor intensive and I was secretly afraid I would catch anthrax.

"You'll have to give her Majesty something else," said Mum sarcastically. I had come up in the world, now I was royalty and no longer the Wee Bitch.

"Boots the chemist has an opening for a cashier," said the woman

"Fine, I'll take her to the shop."

The manager of Boots was a pleasant man and tried to make me feel at ease.

"I'm going to give you some simple additions, percentages, and subtractions."

Simple to him but not me additions, subtractions, multiplications, divisions and percentages rapidly fired at me left me nervous and blank. Math homework had always been Hell for me Mum had absolutely no patience with me from grade one. I knew I was doomed to fail and as he proceeded to give me a list of items at different prices of halfpennies, sixpence, shillings etc. and without the aid of pencil or paper I couldn't remember the price of soap, bandages or rubbing alcohol. As he listed the prices I sweated and mumbled an approximate answer and the change for a five pound note. Wrong!

Mum sat there furious at my stupidity and quickly gave the manager the correct answer, the mystery to me was why she didn't take the job she could have relieved me of my misery? A job may have helped her overcome her endless tirades at home

"You're an idiot! It's hard to believe that you ever went to school," she yelled as we walked home. "What are we going to do with you?"

I believe my mother thought I would turn out to be as lazy as her sister Ruby.

I daily scanned the local newspaper for a job and noticed a vacancy for an office girl in an engineering factory in Gourock, I applied and got the job and for a short time, all seemed well and Mum got off my case. My duties were to make the tea for the office staff, deliver the mail to the post office and to fill in for the switchboard operator when she had her lunch break; unfortunately, the clients for this company were mostly in the north of Scotland and many of them spoke Gaelic. I had great difficulty understanding their broken English; however, this wasn't the reason I left the position it was because of the skirt chasing old boss. Every time I delivered his tea to his desk he cornered me and proceeded to grope under my skirt I was tortured by this bald old coot as he laughed and grabbed my small breasts in his hairy wrinkled fists. It appeared to me that the young women in the office were considered fair game but I was not about to be manhandled. I quit and was ready to face the wrath at home.

That night Dad saved my bacon and decided that since I had top marks in school in typing and shorthand that they would send me to a commercial college to become a secretary. I was so grateful to him because I had visions of ending up working at the rope works or the distillery.

I enrolled in Herd's Commercial School and I loved it. The girls were pleasant and we all had one goal and that was to work in an office and avoid mill work. After completing my courses at the college I noticed an advertisement in the Greenock Telegraph for a Junior Shorthand Typist at the Scott's Shipping Company. I applied and met my future boss who turned out to be the father of my teacher. I was happy and felt confident that I could succeed.

I met my first boyfriend at Scott's he was a friend of my brother John. I had no intention of dating, but an older man in the drafting office bothered me with his pawing fingers and to discourage him I decided I needed a boy friend. At this stage, I was convinced that the older Scotsmen in the offices were all after young tail, as they called it. John suggested I date a tall young man with bright red hair named Hughie; so, I went with him to the pictures and when he tried to kiss me goodnight I quickly told him to get lost. I vowed as I scrubbed my face that night I would never again let any man grope me. Hughie was a kind young man and gave me a canary which spilled its seeds all over the floor, Mum complained about the poor bird and one day it mysteriously flew out the open door never to be seen again. Goodbye Hughie!

Dance halls did not appeal to me because my experiences in them were poor I was tired of men rubbing up against me with an erect penis and smelling of booze; so, I decided to take up ice skating. I sewed a skating skirt, which was probably too short, but as I swished, slid and twirled around the ice I thought I was Sonia Henie. Paisley was a town just a short train ride away from Greenock and had Saturday night ice skating. My brother John was again given the job of looking out for me, but I could shake loose of him. One Saturday night I was particularly good at giving my brothers the slip and they thought I had missed the train, poor Angus was left behind to find me and had to walk over twenty miles home. I was in deep trouble and was left at home for several weeks to teach me a lesson.

Home life was the same and Mum continued her tirades, I was never allowed a friend and every time I brought one home they quickly discovered that they were unwelcome; nevertheless, I did have one friend and we went skating almost every Saturday. Mary was an only child and her parents were very strict, poor Mary wanted to wear a skating skirt; so, she hid it in her bag under her skates and changed when she got to Paisley Ice Rink. Mary's old fashioned mother insisted that she wear warm sensible, heavy knickers and those heavy bloomers slipped below her skating skirt. Very unattractive!

CHAPTER SIXTEEN

When I turned seventeen I had to resign from my job at Scott's because my father was transferred across the River Clyde to Alexandria, Dunbartonshire to the Torpedo Factory. John was still serving his apprenticeship as a Joiner and would have to stay in digs until he was called up to serve in the military.

We moved into a rented house in Balloch, a small town by Loch Lomond. Loch Lomond is probably one of the most beautiful lochs in Scotland. Ben Lomond rises at one end of the loch and the heather covers the hills surrounding this beauty spot. The loch has twelve islands all beginning with the word Inch, one of which is rumored to have a nudist colony. I think they'll all have goose bumps it's so cold out on the loch. In the summer the boat named The Maid of the Loch travels the length of the loch and the tourists arrive by the thousands from Glasgow. Balloch Park is gigantic and full of beautiful flowers and trees my favorite was the Monkey Puzzle Tree (Chilean Pine) the branches swoop down like monkey tails. The park was a great favorite of the locals and in the springtime the walk down the long main drive with the rhododendrons blooming was glorious. At the end of the driveway stood the castle and afforded a magnificent view of Loch Lomond. The village of Balloch was small and catered mainly to the summer visitors with little shops selling souvenirs, ice cream, tea shops and of course the essential fish and chip shop. At the end of the village the River Leven flows by with the water from Loch Lomond all the way to the River Clyde. A favorite of the local teenagers was the dance hall I checked out the local boys; unfortunately, the young men were usually intoxicated and dancing with them proved to be more than I could suffer.

Our new house was located on a corner lot with a gigantic garden which, when the builders had been constructing the houses in the development named Haldane, they had used as a garbage dump. When my Dad decided to create a garden he dug up building materials and bricks by the ton. It was fortunate that my twin brothers were home from the army and they helped him create a rockery surrounding the garden and Mum planted a rose garden on the slope. For a short time she seemed to be happy, we hoped that the change of houses would be good for her.

I had to find another job and I applied to several of the surrounding companies; eventually, I was employed at an aircraft company called Blackburn in the nearby town called Dumbarton. The company made the Venom and the Vampire jet planes and I worked in their main office, my boss was a florid faced bald man who appeared to be overly friendly. I made friends with one of the other girls in the office named Rose and we went to the ice skating together.

Every Saturday we rode the bus to the Erskine Ferry and passed the Erskine Hospital where they cared for the war wounded, then we travelled on to Paisley. As I twirled carefree around the ice wearing my short skating skirt I was unaware that I had attracted a handsome young man.

"Did you make your skating skirt?" he asked.

"Yes," I replied

"My mother is a dressmaker and she would be quite impressed."

"What's your name?" I asked.

"Brian," he said. "You are a super skater."

I knew this was a hyperbole because I was barely able to skate without falling down. I spent more time picking myself off the ice than I did skating on it.

"I saw you on the bus. Do you live in Balloch?" I asked.

"No, I live in Jamestown," he informed me,

"That's close to Balloch."

"Can I take you home?" he asked.

"No, sorry I have to go home with my brother," I said.

"Where do you live and I'll come see you tomorrow?"

I gave him my address and did not expect to ever see him again.

Sunday afternoon I was baking for the family, this was one of my many jobs every weekend, and the door bell rang. There stood Brian dressed in a black blazer and grey flannel trousers and as handsome as Tyrone Power the movie star. Brian was the type of man who wore a tie as soon as he discovered he had a neck; unfortunately, he had made the mistake of arriving on a motorbike and Dad detested the machines. He called them death traps.

"Come in." I said.

"Did you come to take Grace out on a motorbike? Dad asked.

"Yes," he said

"No daughter of mine will ever ride one of those contraptions!"

"That's okay sir, said Brian. "We'll just go for a walk."

We walked through Balloch Park for hours and I found he had a pleasing personality and had spent some of his childhood in England, this explained his accent. His mother was English and widowed and was indeed a dressmaker. He was in his final months in the Air Force and when he was dismissed he intended to join the police force.

I liked him very much and we dated for the weeks he was home on leave. We cycled our bikes all through the glens and by Loch Lomond he was a perfect gentleman and was very different from the Scottish men I had encountered, I willingly kissed him in the backseat of the pictures and I was sure I was in love. Brian was the only boy I had met who used after shaving lotion, other than my teacher Mr. MacCoy, I suppose the rough Scottish lads considered it effeminate; however, Brian was far from girlish I watched him compete in hillside scrambles on his motorbike and he was a fearless rider. Brian did carefree things and one day when we went skating on a frozen pond he jumped onto the ice dressed from head to toe in a skeleton outfit and chased all the girls. He had boundless energy and seemed afraid of nothing he was fun and I felt happy in his company.

My Dad did not like him because he considered any young man without a trade to have no future. One day, Brian took me riding on an old tandem bike that had poor brakes Dad immediately banned him from our house, he was branded as unreliable. I did not expect to ever see him again when he returned home from the Air Force.

Meanwhile, work was becoming increasingly difficult for me because my boss, the old fart, was pushing me every time I entered his office between the filing cabinets and thrusting his fat body against mine. Again, I was confronted with behavior that gave me the creeps. He had a buzzer that he pushed to summon me to his office. I dreaded that buzzer!

Sexual harassment was not considered a problem in the offices and any young female was considered fair game; fortunately, for me all of the men were not like my boss and they decided to help me.

"Let's disconnect Grace's buzzer," said Jimmy, a planning engineer, who worked close to my desk.

Next day my boss was pressing his finger firmly on his buzzer without success.

"Send for an electrician," he demanded.

A young man arrived in the office dressed in overalls carrying a toolbox. I watched him as he repaired my buzzer.

Next day the buzzer was broken again, so the young man again arrived with his tool box.

"I fixed this," he said.

Jimmy smiled and called him to his desk and explained the problem.

He asked, "Who is Grace?

Jimmy pointed to me and suggested to the young man that he get to know me.

When Jimmy told me what he had done I wasn't interested because I still hoped that Brian would eventually pluck up enough courage to come back to my house.

"Brian is not for you, he's not your type, besides he's in the Air Force and Matt is right here," said Jimmy.

Jimmy explained to me that if I had a boyfriend in the factory the old fart would quit bothering me. It had worked before; so, I agreed to see him.

Jimmy became a matchmaker and arranged for me to meet Matt at lunchtime.

I waited for him but he didn't come. I was furious!

"He stood me up!" I said.

"There must be a good reason I'll arrange another meeting," said Jimmy.

This time Matt turned up and apologized and said he had been called away in the factory for an emergency.

I started dating the young electrician named Matt Thomson, the exact same surname as mine. Was this an unlucky omen? The saying goes, change the name and not the letter, change for worse and not for better.

When you first date someone you are oblivious to their faults and overlook many things. He was quiet and appeared to be quite shy, but I was so busy talking that I did not notice that his contribution to the conversation was generally yes, no, or maybe. I can't say it was love at first sight he was a tall very thin young man with brown hair, prominent ears and had false teeth; apparently, his uncle was a dentist and did not believe in fillings only extractions. He was definitely keen to have a girl friend and had never dated before and at dances was refused every dance he asked of the young women because they considered him plain and not handsome enough for them. Sports were his passion he was an avid golfer and played football (soccer) and was attending College and learning electrical work at the factory. His father owned a pub in Alexandria and he was an only child. He was a reliable man and waited every night for me, even in the pouring rain, outside the Vale of Leven Academy School where I was attending classes to finish my education. We walked because neither of us had money for bus fare and I was never in a great hurry to get home. I grew to rely on him and when I introduced him to my family and their first impression of him was good I continued to date him. He was quite at ease with my family and when he offered to help my parents wallpaper the living room walls he was readily accepted. My Dad especially liked the fact that this young man had ambition and plans for his future. I was never sure if he liked him as a person or just the fact that he seemed responsible; however, when Dad found out that his father owned a pub that was definitely a downer, I explained to him that I had never seen Matt drink alcohol he was dubious and found it difficult to believe.

Matt did not skate and when I took him to Paisley he had difficulty keeping his balance so I quit skating and started to go dancing with him or to Glasgow to the pictures.

I continued to look for another job because even with a young boy friend the old fart was a problem and I found one as a stenographer in Alexandria. This job was really better for me because cycling twelve miles per day from Balloch to Dumbarton in the winter was difficult. The company was a textile company called The United Turkey Red and I was the Dye House Manager's secretary. I had my own office and I thought things would be fine although the wages were low; unfortunately, wherever I went there always seemed to be a Mr. Fingers and this one appeared in the dye house laboratory close to my office. At this time in my working career I was tired of the weird old men I had encountered and after one particularly bad day I poured a beaker of blue dye over Mr. Fingers head because he tried to grope me.

"WHAAAT THE HELL!"

Mr. Fingers stood there with blue dye running from his hair over his face and on to his shirt.

"Now you go and explain this to the boss and don't forget to tell him you grabbed my breast!" I screamed.

I expected to be fired but I wasn't, maybe the boss knew Mr. Fingers had a problem; nevertheless, I felt it might be wise to move along sometime soon. Besides the company used a great deal of arsenic in their dyes and as I walked through the puddles of dye every day on my way to my office it splashed on my legs, I knew that arsenic kills and I was afraid it might cause me health problems in later years.

I applied and was hired as a Shorthand Typist at the Royal Naval Torpedo Factory close to my father. At long last, I felt at ease going to work and did not have to fend off the offensive gropers my supervisor was a woman.

CHAPTER SEVENTEEN

If you were to ask the average Scotsman what he thought of Valentine's Day he would probably say, without hesitation that it was a useless waste of money and my boyfriend Matt Thomson was no exception; so, you can imagine my surprise on Valentine's Day when Dad called me, as he was leaving for work, to come to the front door.

I was sound asleep when I heard him yelling. "What the Devil is this blocking the door? Grace, do you know the fool who would do this?"

I reluctantly got out of bed and looked over the banister towards our front door. The door was open but it was completely blocked. A piece of plywood, exactly the same size as the doorway, covered the exit.

Who on earth could have barricaded our door? This obstruction was going to make Dad late for work and because he clocked in being tardy cost money. He proceeded to put his shoulder to the plywood and pushed. It flopped down on the pathway.

Dad picked up the wood, turned it over and stood it up against the brick wall. Then I heard him laughing.

"Come here lass there's a gift for you," he said. "Someone has brought you a Valentine."

It was a freezing winter morning and yet I felt a warm glow as I stared in amazement at this token of love. It was incredible! Who could have secretly delivered this gigantic card to my doorstep?

In bold black letters a short verse read:

"GRACE, GRACE, WITH THE PRETTY FACE, I LOVE YOU!"

Painted pink hearts, naked cupids, ruby red roses, bows and kisses had been carefully created by some fanciful lad. It was a work of art and whoever had painted this was talented. I was flattered but also a little embarrassed, the problem was our house was very close to the bus stop and the art was illuminated by our outside lights. The bus driver had stopped the bus so that the passengers could view the Valentine and the passengers who knew me were laughing.

That day I went to work and, as anticipated, I was teased. The teasing wasn't bad but I wondered if any of the jokers were responsible for my funny Valentine.

After tea Dad chopped my gift for kindling, the card was useful and provided us with warmth. Throughout the winter I often watched the little pieces of cupid burn and I felt quite sad watching the flames consume this declaration of love.

I never found out who brought my Valentine but I did know that Brian was back in town. To this day it remains a mystery.

My brother John was called up to the army but before he went he met Matt just once and immediately liked him. This was a good omen for me I trusted John's judgment more than anyone else.

Matt and I decided to become engaged, but before this happened I would have to meet his parents. I wasn't sure of this because I had heard that his mother was a special lady and looked and acted like the Queen Mother. I dreaded the day I would have to meet her.

I dressed in my best outfit; unfortunately, I had only one pair of nylon stockings and they had a gigantic rip right up the front of the leg. When I reached the corner of their street and looked across at their beautiful home I froze.

"I can't go in there that's where the toffs live!" I whispered.

"Don't be crazy my folks will like you."

I was about to run when his father came to the door and waved. I was sunk I had to cross the street.

"Hello, come on in," he invited.

I entered their house and was stunned. I knew that pub owners were not poor but this was ridiculous. The display cabinets were jammed with silver and fine bone china. The furniture was plush and the carpets were thick and lush. The entire house reeked of money—booze is certainly a lucrative business.

His mother was sitting by a large fire doing fine embroidery and stood up as I entered. Later, I discovered that she was indeed a creative woman and designed all the patterns for her embroidery. Before marrying she had been a silk screen designer and was quite artistic.

"Nice to meet you, we've heard so much about you from Matt," she said quietly.

I sat stiffly trying to hide my ripped stockings throughout the entire afternoon. I was completely ill at ease beside this lovely woman who was obviously trying very hard to make me feel comfortable. I looked at her display cabinet of silver in awe and muttered.

"Someone has won a great many trophies."

"Oh! That's not trophies dear that's a silver tea service," she explained

I had never seen a silver tea service in my life we had just recently bought a china tea set from the money my Dad had won on the football coupons. I was clearly out of my depth and upon leaving their house I endeavored to explain to Matt that this would never work.

"You need to find a new girl friend I'll never be accepted by your family," I told him

"Rubbish, they don't count!"

"Oh! Yes they do. I can't marry you!" I told him.

I left Matt by the bridge in tears and ran home I was sure I would never see him again after all we had lots of time to find the right partner he was twenty and I was just eighteen. We were apart for less than a week and once again we were a couple trying to grow up enough to understand our feelings.

Summer holidays arrived and, I thought, since I would be going on a Youth Hostel cycling holiday with my family perhaps if Matt spent some time with them he would probably run for his life.

"Would you like to go on a cycling holiday with my family?" I asked.

"Sure, I'd love to," he replied eagerly.

A cycling holiday was not a "holiday" with us it was an endurance test. My Dad and Mum were now riding their new Flying Scot tandem with ten gears. My twin brothers also had feather light bikes with light pannier bags and John and I had heavy tanks loaded down with pannier bags. My Dad's idea was that he would bring us up the hard way. From the oldest to the youngest we all had to prove we could take whatever the weather had to offer and whatever the terrain we travelled without complaints. This we did not mind but added to this was my Mum's temper which could explode at any moment.

Poor unsuspecting Matt arrived with his heavy bike prepared to spend an enjoyable holiday with the girl he hoped to marry. Our destination was Oban about a week's travel by bike. Youth hostels could be primitive and sometimes they had outside toilets, army issue bunks, cold water for baths and communal cooking facilities. The roads we travelled to reach the hostels were narrow with pot holes and many of them mountainous. If we dismounted it was considered wimpy we pedaled from early morning to dusk stopping only to eat by the roadside. Matt did it without complaint, in fact he seemed to relish whatever was dished out to him, he had been in the Boy's Brigade for years and loved to camp. Half way to Oban, Mum had her first meltdown. We stopped at a park to shelter in a gazebo from the pelting rain. Mum decided to lie out in the grass without a raincoat. I stood quietly waiting beside Matt.

Suddenly, she stood up dripping wet and walked towards us we were unsure of what to say or do. No explanation was given, none was expected, we just mounted our bikes and travelled on but I felt that Matt was considerably ill at ease from that day until the end of the trip.

The holiday seemed endless, fourteen days of staying in Spartan hostels, eating truly awful food, foul weather and feeling unsure of the company. I was certain I would probably never see Matt again after the holiday if this was a sample of what to expect should he marry into this family it would be too much for any prospective suitor. When we reached Oban I expected Matt to buy a train ticket home and vanish but instead we spent the day alone and it was heavenly.

A week later Matt, like the proverbial bad penny, turned up and asked me to the pictures, I wasn't sure if he felt sorry for me or did this young man truly love me? Whatever it was about Matt he certainly seemed to have staying power and maybe his declaration of love for me was true.

I continued to see his parents and discovered that his father had been a professional football (soccer) and played for Preston North End, in the English First Division. He introduced me to his extended family of aunts and uncles and they turned out to be really extraordinary and genuinely nice people.

Matt decided when he was twenty-one and I was nineteen he would again ask me to marry him and I gladly accepted. We went to Glasgow and picked out rings; afterwards, we went to the pictures and saw "Friendly Persuasion" starring Gary Cooper. The theme song was sung by Pat Boone. It became our song.

We drove home to my parent's house dreading the scene that would ensue when I told them I was engaged.

"You wait here in the car and I'll go tell them," I begged.

"No, we'll tell them together," said Matt.

"Trust me I know what I'm doing."

So, I entered the lion's den and waited for the roar.

"I'm engaged to marry Matt Thomson," I timidly told them.

"No, you're not!" Dad said. "Give him the ring back. I won't allow you to marry a publican's son. I hate the bastards!"

Mum said nothing, I couldn't believe it I expected an outburst from her.

I ran from the house and jumped back into the car.

"I'm sorry my Dad said I have to give you the ring back. I can't marry you," I said.

I handed him the ring and he was shocked. "Why?"

"He said he won't allow me to marry a publican's son. My Dad has a real hatred of everything connected to alcohol," I explained.

"That's ridiculous! I don't drink booze and neither does my Dad we don't drink our profits," Matt sounded really angry.

"That's the problem. Dad thinks that publican's are responsible for his miserable childhood," I sobbed and gulped down my tears.

"It's not the man who sells the alcohol to blame it's the responsibility of the drinker to know when he's had enough," said Matt.

"I'm sorry Matt, I can't explain. My Dad has his mind dead set against anything connected with alcohol. I can't marry you."

Out of the car he leapt, charging up our pathway, banging on our door, it opened and he entered my house. I sat there petrified, I thought he'd come back probably with a black eye.

Minutes went by and still he did not appear; finally, the door opened and he sauntered back to the car and handed me back my solitaire diamond ring.

"We're engaged and with no objections," he said triumphantly.

We were engaged in March and little did I know that in April we would be parted.

CHAPTER EIGHTEEN

"I'm going to Canada," my fiancée said happily.

"You're what!" I was stunned.

"My parents don't want me to go to the military and I'm leaving for Canada in April."

I stood there amazed!, we were newly engaged and he was taking off to Canada. I stared at my engagement ring and wondered if this was this their way of breaking the engagement? It seemed like an expensive break it would have been easier to send him to Ireland.

"What about me?"

"Oh! You can come in a year or two once I get settled. I'm going to live with my Uncle George he owns an oil company in Edmonton, Alberta," said Matt.

"My God, if you think it was difficult for me to become engaged to you and you were staying in Scotland, what do you think will happen if I tell my parents that we're going to Canada?" I asked. "I don't care if your uncle owns Shell Oil it's just out of the question."

"I have no choice my parents have bought the ticket, I sail on the Empress of Scotland. First class ticket, how about that!" Matt said jubilantly.

"Yeah, how about that," I said dumb struck.

"My Dad will come over and explain to your folks the arrangements," said Matt.

"Are you mad, my Dad will chase him he doesn't stand a chance of explaining to my parents they just will not understand."

"Oh sure they will," Matt said confidently.

Arrangements were made for the parents to meet and explanations given as to why my parent's future son-in-law would be a draft dodger.

Part of the explanation given to them was that Matt's father had been in the British Army throughout World War II and considered it one of the worst experiences of his life. During his service his wife had had to work in the pub and the care of his young son Matt was given over to his grandmother and maiden aunt.

"This isn't a good enough explanation why your son doesn't serve. He doesn't have a pub or a wife and child."

"Well that's not the only reason I don't want my boy connected with anything military," said Matt's father.

"What other reason do you have?" Dad asked.

"There are too many homosexuals in the forces," he attempted to explain.

"What!"

"That's right, I saw them when I served and I bloody well don't want my boy exposed to that side of life," he said emphatically. Matt's father was fluent in curse words.

My father was unable to substantiate the explanation given to him as to whether this was true or false. The subject of sexual preference was never discussed in our family neither his brothers nor sons had ever talked about homosexuals in the military.

"What about my daughter, she's engaged to young Matt?" Dad asked.

"In a year or less Matt's mother will take her to Canada to marry him," Matt's father assured him.

A week before my twentieth birthday I said goodbye to Matt as he sailed away from Greenock, I watched him leave the dock by tender and waved until my arm ached, I realized how much I loved this pragmatic young man. In matters of the heart nobody can tell the future. He sailed away to Canada not knowing what lay ahead. His poor mother cried until she was exhausted. His father stood there stoically and never shed a tear. Maybe Matt was right when he said he suspected that his father wanted rid of him. Who knew what purpose they had in sending their only son into exile?

That night I went to the dancing in Gourock with my brother Duncan and fiancée Annie. They planned to wed that June and I was to be their bridesmaid. Annie was a Merino Mill girl and admirable suited to my brother Duncan, they were like two peas in a pod. Duncan, the quiet and supposedly unassuming twin and Annie the girl who basically said nothing of any consequence and appeared to cause no problem for my mother had met at the Paisley skating and, since Duncan was almost thirty, it was high time he wed. Angus had also met a mill girl and would wed a year after his brother, her name was Hannah and she rarely spoke, wise girl! If she had an opinion she never

ever voiced it; thereby, also staying out of trouble with my mother.

I continued to work at the Torpedo Factory beside my father and since I was to be Annie's bridesmaid I had to buy a suitable dress. Every penny was a prisoner for me I was saving for my own wedding in Canada.

Before the wedding my mother had several meltdowns and life at home was intolerable, whenever anything out of the norm was happening at home the stress became too much for her and she had suicidal thoughts. One of our neighbors had been found drowned in the River Leven; apparently, the poor woman had decided suicide was the only answer to whatever problems she had, discarding her fur coat, purse and shoes by the riverbank she waded in and drowned. This incident started my mother on one of her newest ideas—drowning. She threatened that instead of wading into the water that she would throw herself off the bridge. When she found that wasn't getting the desired results from the family throwing herself in front of the train became her next threat. We lived in a state of dread.

The wedding eve arrived and we all travelled to Greenock. I was to stay with Hannah's family and I was told to bar my door because the father was prone to sleep walking and entered rooms without permission. I had a sleepless night!

The wedding was delightful, the bride was quite lovely. I wore a yellow dress, the color choice of the bride. At the reception, I again met the "kitten killer" he came with our old neighbor Mrs. White he told me he planned to emigrate to Australia because; unfortunately, his young bride had died. I didn't ask the cause of her death but my imagination went wild.

Meanwhile, I continued to see Matt's parents and they were extremely kind to me. I had tea with them every week and they took me to the pictures. They were anxious for news of their son because he was not writing to them as often as he wrote me I was happy to fill in the blanks for them.

Matt had met his Uncle George in Edmonton, Alberta and found that the man was definitely not an oil tycoon instead he was barely scraping by financially. He owned a re-refining business in the seediest part of town; basically, he took dirty oil and extracted the muck and sold it to local farmers for their tractors. He lived in a flop house and slept on a couch, warmed his food on a hot plate, and lived like a tinker. Matt was sadly disillusioned because he had anticipated an uncle with great wealth. It's not uncommon for people, when they go abroad, to write to their families of their great fortunes. Of course, I was told never to divulge this information to Matt's mother or grandmother, it was best for them if they continued to think that Uncle George was a great success. I believe that, judging from Matt's correspondence regarding his Uncle George that he now considered himself to be a success and a very happy man. Apparently, George was a teenager when he arrived in Edmonton hoping to join his grandmother's family who owned a farm. They had worked him like a slave, paid him very little, and when he complained they threw him out. Another family saga of lies and deceit!

Matt when he first went to Edmonton stayed in one of the flop house rooms beside George it was a definitely a step down from his comfortable home in Scotland. Matt decided as soon as he found employment he would move. One day, he noticed an advertisement in the Edmonton Journal for an engineering draftsman for Alberta Government Telephones he applied and was fortunate to meet Harold MacKay, the son of a Scotsman, who gladly gave him the job.

Things were moving along nicely, surely my father would have no objections to me leaving Scotland now that Matt had secured a government job. Boy was I wrong! My father had no intention of parting with his only daughter and threw every roadblock in my way short of tying me to my bed. Once again, my brother John came to my rescue and told my father that if he didn't let me go as promised that, when I turned twenty-one and of legal age, I would probably go without their permission and they would never see me again. This I believe convinced Dad to let me go.

Wedding presents arrived for us from my uncles and aunts and they came to say goodbye. My parents were aghast at the gifts and knew that I did not have the money to ship them to Canada; so, instead of them paying for my wedding they paid for the shipment of twenty-seven tablecloths, tray cloths, tea pots, tea sets, cutlery, etc. My sister-in-law gave me an expandable suitcase and I packed every warm garment I owned, I had read Matt's letters and expected thirty below zero in the winter time. I carefully packed my wedding gown that I had purchased weeks before in Glasgow it was like a ballerina's dress with an embroidered top and soft flowing skirt with many layers of satin and net. I still had one hundred and fifty pounds not a lot but it had taken me a year to save it.

CHAPTER NINETEEN

The day arrived and, as promised, Matt's mother was escorting me to Canada. We drove to Prestwick Airport in Ayrshire we were flying on a prop job the Super Constellation. At the airport there were many tears and hugs, I believe my parents thought they would never see me again. I hugged my tearful Mum this woman I could never see through but in her fashion she had seen me through many ups and downs. As I crossed the tarmac to enter the plane I turned around and saw them all waving, then I heard my father playing his harmonica, he was playing one of my favorite Scottish tunes "Scotland the Brave". Maybe my father was telling me, his young Scottish daughter, to be brave. The road that lay ahead of me in Canada was a mystery but I knew I was up to the challenge; after all, I grew up the hard way.

Recipe for Mum's Clootie Dumpling (Clootie means cloth)

2 cups flour, 1 cup raisins, 1 cup currants, ¾ cup brown sugar, 1 cup beef kidney suet,
2 teaspoons all spice, ½ teaspoon cinnamon, ½ teaspoon nutmeg, 1 tablespoon baking powder, 6 slices finely grated bread, 1 egg, 1 cup milk.

Method: Mix all the dry ingredients in a large bowl. Add milk and egg. Mix with a wooden spoon to give a stiff consistency. Set aside. Wet and lightly flour a clean cotton towel or a 24" square piece of white cloth (do not use a terry towel). Place the mixture in the center of the towel and gather all the ends together leaving 2" for expansion of the dumpling. Tie tightly with strong string. Make absolutely certain that there is no space to allow water inside. Place an old small plate in a large soup pot (prevents dumpling from sticking to the bottom of pot), pour 6 cups of water into the pot and bring to a boil. Turn down heat keeping the water at a simmer. Lower the dumping onto the plate. The water should be approximately half way up the sides of the dumping. Check often to make sure that it does not boil dry, add a little hot water from time to time. Simmer for four hours. Remove the dumpling from the pot and carefully peel the cloth from the dumpling. Set oven to 200 degrees F. Turn dumpling onto a cake pan. Place the dumpling in the oven for approximately 30 minutes, or until the dumpling feels dry and not sticky.

Serve warm with custard or slice and eat as fruit cake. Also, next day when the dumpling is cold it can be reheated by frying it in vegetable oil until gently browned.